THE ROSETTA STONE
AND THE REBIRTH OF ANCIENT EGYPT

WONDERS OF THE WORLD

....

THE ROSETTA STONE
AND THE REBIRTH OF
ANCIENT EGYPT

JOHN RAY

Harvard University Press
Cambridge, Massachusetts
2007

First published in the United Kingdom by
Profile Books Ltd
3A Exmouth House
Pine S treet
London EZ1R OJH, U.K.

Typeset in Caslon by MacGuru Ltd
info@macguru.org .uk
Designed by Peter Campbell

Printed in the United States of America

Library of Congress Cataloging-in-Publication Data

Ray, J. D.
The Rosetta Stone and the rebirth of ancient Egypt / John Ray.
p. cm. — (Wonders of the World)
ISBN-13: 978-0-674-02493-9 (alk. paper)
ISBN-10: 0-674-02493-1 (alk. paper)
1. Rosetta stone. 2. Egyptian language—Writing.
3. Egyptology—History. I. Title.
PJ1531.R5R39 2007
493'.1—dc22   2007001834

For Sonia
'But I don't suppose we'll meet'
(Luxor, January 1990)

CONTENTS

1. The Rosetta Stone as it is today, on display in the British Museum.

INTRODUCTION

The Rosetta Stone is the most famous object in the British Museum. According to the museum's own figures, it is the most visited item in the entire display, and perhaps the most lingered over, although a similar claim is sometimes made for the unwrapped mummy of a ginger tomcat which also forms part of the Egyptian collections. The stone is one of the world's wonders, although it does not feature in the conventional lists of Wonders of the World. It is not a monumental building, but it attracts pilgrims in the way that imposing ruins do. In mundane reality it was part of a mass-produced series of stelae, a technical term for slabs of stone designed to perpetuate the official records of the Egyptian state. What it records is a decree, the text of an agreement issued jointly by a king and a synod of ancient Egyptian clergy. Its purpose was to witness to the Pharaoh's benevolence towards his people and his piety towards the gods. It was the sort of thing a good king was expected to do, and to go on doing.

According to the inscription on the stone, an identical copy of the decree was to be placed in every sizeable temple in the land. Whether this really happened is impossible to say, but a few copies of the same trilingual decree have been found and can be seen in other museums. The version that we have is some 112 centimetres high and 76 centimetres

2. The Rosetta Stone as it was originally: modern reconstruction by Richard Parkinson and colleagues at the British Museum.

wide, but the original stone was considerably taller than it is today. Its uppermost register would have been decorated with figures of the king and the gods of the temple where it stood. These are long gone. Of the hieroglyphic text which formed its second register, only a third is left. The hieroglyphs were the most important of the scripts on the stone; they were there for the gods to read, and the more learned of their priesthood. The grammar and vocabulary of this section of the decree were scarcely changed from what they would have been 2,000 years earlier. The Greek text which forms the bottom register has also lost one of its corners. Since the arrival of Alexander the Great in 332 BC, Egypt was ruled by the dynasty of the Ptolemies, who carried on the title of Pharaoh, although Greek was now the language of government. However, in the hierarchical world of Egyptian temples, this Johnny-come-lately script, a miserable alphabet with no more than twenty-four signs and no religious connotations whatsoever, had no choice but to remain on the bottom row. The inscription above the Greek register is the best preserved, but even this is not complete. It is composed in demotic, a form of hieroglyphic shorthand which was the standard script for day-to-day affairs in the Egypt of the Ptolemies, and which was closest to the spoken language of most of the population.

The Rosetta Stone lay for centuries in the ruins of its temple, perhaps in the city of Sais or somewhere else in the Nile Delta. At some point what remained of it was reused as building material, since its long-silent inscriptions could no longer be read. It may not have reached the town of Rosetta until the later part of the fifteenth century, when the fort into which it was recycled was constructed. It lay buried in this fort until the summer of 1799, when the French, who had invaded Egypt the previous year, restructured the building as part of their efforts to secure the coast. The French officers sensed that the stone was something extraordinary. Off it went to Cairo, and the attentions of Napoleon's think-tank, the savants of the so-called Institut d'Égypte. But its existence among the French was to be short-lived, since it was destined to fall into the hands of their arch-enemy, the British.

The day may come when the stone has spent longer in the British Museum than it ever did in Rosetta. Since its arrival in the museum as spoils of war in June 1802, it has never left its adopted home, apart from being moved to shelter during the two World Wars. There was also a brief visit to Paris in 1972, to celebrate a centenary and a half of its decipherment. The press at the time made much of the possibility that the unscrupulous French were preparing to kidnap it. Nothing of the sort occurred, and it is now back in the Egyptian galleries. For a part of its history in the museum it was displayed without a glass cover, so that visitors could touch its surface. Nowadays this is not encouraged, but the museum has enterprisingly placed a replica in the King's Library for those who feel the need to run their hands over the inscriptions. It is as if this ancient piece of granite has become the modern version of a religious relic.

Religious relics in the Middle Ages were a centre for the tourist industry, and they spawned replicas and souvenirs. The stone is no exception. There are postcards, facsimiles, booklets and imitations everywhere on sale. Figures given by the British Museum itself confirm that, over the years, and as long as museum staff can remember, a plain postcard of the

Rosetta Stone has been the best-selling item in its souvenir bookshop. As postcards go, it is devoid of action and almost monochrome, since all it shows is a piece of lead-coloured rock covered with whitish signs that must be unintelligible to most of the people who buy it. This is not the point: visitors to the museum clearly feel the need to own something of the stone, and to take it home with them or share it with their friends. It is as if the museum and the stone are interchangeable, and the stone has become the part which can stand for the whole building and its wealth of collections. More substantial than a postcard, a small rubber version of the stone is the mouse pad which is helping me write this introduction. Such things are the takeaway equivalents of the pieces of cloth which have touched a famous icon or a bone of one of the Apostles.

The stone can readily be called iconic. It is an icon of Egyptology, since it gave birth to that science. It is an icon of genius, since its mysteries attracted two formidable intellects, one English and one French. Thomas Young and Jean-François Champollion are two of the most remarkable minds of the Napoleonic age, and the differences between them are equally revealing. But icons can be fought over. The stone may have hoped to bring understanding and civilisation to future ages, but it has also proved capable of spreading division and recriminations. During the lifetimes of Young and Champollion, there were many who tried to set these two men against each other. After their deaths a feud intensified between their respective supporters which at times started to look like a replay of the Napoleonic Wars. A keeper (admittedly one from the Channel Islands) at no less an institution than the British Museum itself had the audacity to belittle the great Thomas Young in print, and several modern writers seem to regard the English scientist as the Mr Hyde of the Rosetta Stone: an embittered prima donna who went out of his way to make difficulties for his younger colleague across the Channel. Even now, the issue of who did what first and who owed which insight to the other is capable of flaring up again, and there is no shortage of people who want to use the hieroglyphs to stage a rerun of Waterloo. When the stone made its 1972 trip to Paris, it was exhibited alongside a picture of Jean-François Champollion and another of Thomas Young. There were complaints from some of the French that the portrait of Young was larger than that of his rival, and there were cries of outrage from the other side that the portrait of the Frenchman was manifestly bigger than that of Young. Both portraits had been chosen carefully and they were exactly the same size.

The stone may be part of an ancient past, but it is also an icon of the modern world, since it gave us back one of the longest and most romantic chapters of our history, a chapter which had been thought lost beyond recall. To recover past memory is to regain identity. The Rosetta Stone is, in effect, an emblem of our identity. A company that makes software for learning languages markets itself under the name Rosetta Stone, and a search of the internet for the words 'Rosetta Stone' manages to prove illuminating and disconcerting at the same time. Almost any breakthrough in knowledge, or a new slant on an old concept, can acquire the name, and some of the twists and connotations are as hard to decipher as the hieroglyphs themselves. A European project to investigate comets in deep space has been termed the Rosetta Mission. A versatile group of chamber musicians goes under the name the Rosetta Trio, presumably because there are three of them, and three is the number of languages on the stone. There is even a Japanese glam rock group which calls itself Rosetta Stone, and *The Rosetta Stone* turns out to be the title of an animated film, the fifth in a series of mysteries solved by the world-famous dog detective, Sherlock Hound. What the stone tells us about ourselves seems to be as important as what it tells us about events which happened long ago. It brought about more than a decipherment: it is the key to decipherment itself.

The stone has its own history. It was created in ancient Egypt, and it has restored to us the story and the literature of this most glamorous of civilisations. Before its discovery, most of what was known about Egypt was erroneous, with scholars labouring under the misconception that everything to do with the country was a lost, impenetrable mystery. Its discovery brought about a revolution in our knowledge of how writing works, and its origins. It was fought, or quarrelled, over by two superpowers, and even now the question of who owns it, or who ought to own it, is an important one. The stone, if we listen to it carefully, may be telling us about our future as well as our past.

I first visited the British Museum as a schoolboy, on 1 April 1958. We had been given a half-day holiday. There were the mummies, the unwrapped and bedraggled tom, the sarcophagi and the large facsimiles on the walls of the Book of the Dead of the scribe Ani. Ginger, the curled-up predynastic man, was there in his remade burial, and the colossal head of Ramesses II, 'the younger Memnon', smiled, serene and self-satisfied, over the sculpture gallery. There too was the Rosetta Stone, which a few days earlier had silently celebrated its 2,154th birthday, judging from the fact that the lines of its trilingual text are dated to 27 March 196 BC. In the museum bookshop (much smaller then than it is today) I bought a short monograph on the stone, written by one of the museum's most famous curators, Sir E. A. Wallis Budge. It was a distinctly dry publication, already decades old, and the museum has long since come up with more stylish replacements. But it was the first academic work of Egyptology that the schoolboy acquired, and it did its bit to start him on his career. I knew that I wanted what the Stone was trying to tell me. As one of the best writers in the English language for 12½-year-olds of all ages put it:

> Where among the desert sands
> Some deserted city stands,
> All its children, sweep and prince,
> Grown to manhood ages since,
> Not a foot in street or house,
> Not a stir of child or mouse,
> And when kindly falls the night,
> In all the town no spark of light.
> There I'll come when I'm a man
> With a camel caravan;
> Light a fire in the gloom
> Of some dusty dining-room;
> See the pictures on the walls,
> Heroes, fights and festivals;
> And in a corner find the toys
> Of the old Egyptian boys.

Robert Louis Stevenson, *A Child's Garden of Verses*, 'Travel' (1885)

I

....

THE FADING OF THE LIGHT

*All is thus here – the women wail the dead, as on the old sculp-
tures; they offer sacrifices to the Nile, and walk round ancient
statues in order to have children. The ceremonies at births and
burials are not Muslim, but ancient Egyptian ... This country is
a palimpsest, in which the Bible is written over Herodotus, and
the Koran over that.*

Lucy Duff Gordon, letter from Egypt, February 1863

The island of Philae lies in the Nile on the tropic of Cancer,
near the ancient frontier between Egypt and Nubia. The
Philae which is visited by modern tourists is in reality a reconstruction caused by the building of the Aswan High Dam in
the early 1960s, but the stones of the ancient temples were
painstakingly transferred to their new site on another island
and faithfully rebuilt. On the site of Philae, the goddess Isis
was once worshipped for more than seven centuries, and
pilgrims from the whole of Egypt, Nubia and parts of the
Mediterranean world paid pilgrimage to her there. A single
tear from the goddess's eye as she mourned her dead husband,
Osiris, was believed to fall into the river late in every July, and
the result was the inundation of the Nile. On the walls of her
temple there are inscriptions in Greek, in Meroitic (the still-

3. The island of Philae, in its original location at the First Cataract.

undeciphered language of a Sudanese kingdom which rivalled Rome for control of the Nile) and in the age-old language of the hieroglyphs. In addition to the temple inscriptions, some of the Egyptian texts are written in demotic, and these take the form of pious graffiti, the records of pilgrims visiting the sacred places. The temples themselves have their hymns and rituals recorded in hieroglyphs, since, as the Rosetta Stone itself puts it, these sacred pictures were 'the writing of the words of the gods'. When the Rosetta Stone was composed, early in the second century BC, there seemed to be no reason why the same gods would not continue to speak for ever, even if they now permitted their country to be governed in Greek. The gods of the hieroglyphs had created Egypt and it followed that they would never cease to protect it.

In a corner of the island of Philae, on the wall of a chapel dedicated to the Nubian god Mandulis, there is an inscription in the same hieroglyphic script, put there by a scribe of the sacred writings. A demotic graffito accompanying the text dates it to 24 August in the year AD 394. The hieroglyphs are crude compared with most of the texts from the site and a romantically inclined visitor can imagine that they had been carved when the light was fading. We will never know the time of day when these hieroglyphs were written, but we do not need to. The light that was fading when this text was composed was the light of knowledge. These are the last hieroglyphs that were carved in Egypt. Christianity had come to the Roman Empire and the old gods were falling silent.

The change of religion had a profound consequence for Egyptians. They still lived among the monuments of their past, which are some of the most impressive on earth. But the gods and the spirits of the dead who inhabited the temples

4. The last hieroglyphs, on the wall of the chapel of Mandulis at Philae.

and tombs were no longer theirs to revere: they had become demonic, something alien which could be feared but should not be approached. Nor could they be studied, since they were dangerous. A later Christian hermit took refuge in the tomb of Ramesses IV in the Valley of the Kings, living alone among the figures which had been painted on its walls more than a millennium and a half before his day. Just inside the entrance he left an inscription in red ink in Coptic, the descendant of the old language of the Pharaohs, which was now written in a version of the Greek alphabet. He tells us how he was driven to cover up the inscriptions he could see around him, because he was terrified of the power of the words they contained. He could not read them, but he knew that they were capable of taking over his thoughts and cutting him off from his God. An Egyptologist is the last thing this nervous monk would have wanted to be.

The degree to which knowledge of the past was lost can be seen in Egypt today. Egyptians are proud of their history, and they take all possible care of their heritage, but no Egyptian would dream of claiming that he or she was a direct descendant of any of the Pharaohs. Genetically, there may still be unbroken links, because the population has remained remarkably stable over the centuries, and the number of foreign settlers has been quite limited. But whether Christian or Muslim, no modern Egyptian would gain anything by claiming that the blood of Ramesses or Queen Hatshepsut flowed in his or her veins. The anonymous Pharaoh who appears in the Qur'an is a figure of godless arrogance. The Pharaoh who appears in modern Arabic schoolbooks is different, in that he is no longer nameless and is part of a glorious past; but it is a past that is inaccessible, and therefore safe.

The direct link with the past was severed, and it continued that way even after the coming of the Arabs in the seventh century. The records of the old religion were no longer required. As knowledge of hieroglyphs and their demotic equivalents died away, papyri were no longer preserved and recopied, and temples which were not turned into churches were left to decay, or treated as convenient quarries for ready-cut stone. Statues of gold, silver or bronze were melted down, and their inscriptions perished in the process, although the metal itself was recycled. The answer to the question which an Egyptologist so often hears, 'What became of all that gold they had?', is that the questioner is probably wearing some of it in his or her watch or jewellery.

Christian, or Coptic, Egypt was part of the Byzantine Empire, although it turned its back on that empire by its adoption of a differing form of Christianity, one which emphasised Jesus' single nature, combining human and divine in one indivisible whole. Relations with the capital, Constantinople, remained grudging, and there were times when political allegiance came close to breaking down. The Arabs were welcomed with some relief by the majority of Egypt's population when they invaded in AD 640, and the Islamic conquest met with little resistance. One of the consequences of this peaceful takeover was that the new overlords were free to turn their curiosity to the wonders that the country still possessed. The Arab conquerors took over the richer and more sophisticated half of the Roman Empire. Here, for 1,000 years, most of the intellectual life had been conducted in Greek rather than Latin. Arabic scholars lost no time translating works of Greek philosophy and science, in many cases preserving sources of knowledge which were lost in medieval Europe or which never reached the West at all. The same to a lesser extent turns out to be true of ancient Egypt.

Until recently it was usual to treat the Arabic contribution to ancient Egypt as a fantasy on a theme rather than the theme itself. The Rosetta Stone was still slumbering in the earth of the Delta, and the medieval historians were almost as much in the dark as the stone was. But we can now turn to a brave attempt to rehabilitate their efforts. Okasha El Daly, an Egyptian scholar based in London, has collected the Arabic material in a book entitled *Egyptology: The Missing Millennium*. This book shows that the Arabic writers had access to accounts and traditions about the ancient world which are much more detailed than we imagined, and which in some cases may go back to seriously good authorities.

In the Arabic writers there are accounts of ancient temples, mummies both human and animal, gilded idols and copies of ancient texts written in hieroglyphic, demotic or Coptic, with attempts at translation. There is much on ancient astrology, although this practice does not seem to have been known in Egypt before the country was incorporated into the intercontinental empire of the Persians in 525 BC. A king named Tosidon or Tomidon (possibly one of the Greek Ptolemies) is said to have had a glass planetarium. An anonymous queen built a temple on the walls of which all manner of armies were portrayed. When a particular type invaded, she simply went to the temple and obliterated the appropriate picture or pictures, thus putting a stop to the invasion. A king named Ashmun is described as building a tunnel under the Nile, its walls covered with coloured glass, so that his royal ladies could cross to the sun temple on the other bank without getting wet. In reality,

Ashmun is the name of a place rather than a person, but the story is too good to spoil with pedantic details.

Above all, this material returns and returns to the two obsessions of the medieval Near East: magic and buried treasure. Sometimes the two themes can be cleverly combined. The distinctly unorthodox eleventh-century ruler Al-Hakim (who came from a Shi'ite dynasty, the Fatimids) is said in one gossipy account to have employed an ancient idol which housed a familiar spirit. This spirit from the remote past could reveal the whereabouts of stolen objects, a technique which enabled the sovereign to be tough on thieving and tough on the causes of thieving, at least by anyone except himself.

Other sources preserved by Arabic writers deal with medicine, astronomy and the wisdom of the sage Hermes, who is sometimes described as Hermes the Copt. Here it is clear that the Greek and Roman admiration of the Egyptians as herbalists and alchemists (a word which derives from *Khemi*, the Coptic name for Egypt itself) continued well into post-classical times. Equally intriguing is the way that ideas from the ancient past survived beyond the coming of Islam. We can read in the historian Al-Idrisi that even in his time (he died in 1251) there was a particular day in the year when people who hoped for preferment from the Sultan would offer incense to the Sphinx. Egyptians, pagan, Christian and Muslim, had been doing this for the better part of three millennia when Al-Idrisi wrote these words. The link with written history may have been broken, but the traces of deeper patterns of behaviour remained. It is these deeper patterns which the Victorian traveller Lucy Duff Gordon noticed, in the letter quoted at the beginning of this chapter.

Much of this Arabic literature comes from Coptic sources, either written or verbal, since medieval Egyptians were well aware that Coptic was the direct descendant of the ancient language. They also went in awe of Coptic priests and others who were believed to have access to the secrets of the long-dead past, and they will have consulted magicians, and other 'alternative' practitioners who would have preferred to remain anonymous, given that what they were doing could carry serious penalties. Some of this material does seem to contain real information about the past, but the rest of it is likely to be the product of folklore or wishful thinking rather than factual research. It is not difficult to believe that Coptic sources preserve some accurate memories. A detailed account of Pharaonic taxation which is preserved in the fifteenth-century work of Ibn Zahira may turn out to rest on secure foundations, and the same is likely to be true of the sources describing Alexandria and its various marvels. These may well have survived in Greek manuscripts.

The truth is that the Copts were ambiguous about their Pharaonic ancestors. Their religion, and the monuments which it produced, could only be the product of worshipping false gods, mummifying animals, dabbling with the occult and other abominations. As such, it had to be anathema, something forbidden. But the forbidden was horribly attractive. How could such a misguided past produce a civilisation which was greater than the present? What power or powers drove it, and brought it into being? The more the ancient culture was thought to be deluded, and in the grip of demons, the more the curiosity fed on itself. It is this fascination with the forbidden and the exotic which helped to preserve it, and which is passed down in the Arabic writers.

For some people, this elaborate material about the ancient past amounts to Egyptology in something like the modern sense. If Egyptology is defined as a fascination with all things Pharaonic and a curiosity about what this civilisation achieved, then we can say that Egyptology is what we are dealing with here. But if Egyptology is to be seen as a historical science, we will have to conclude that many of the Arabic sources fall short of this. Their attempts to read individual hieroglyphs and to give them phonetic values were wide of the mark, although the recognition that there was a phonetic side to hieroglyphs was an important one, which will recur in the next few chapters. The names of kings such as Ashmun and many of the gods given in the Arabic writers are unrecognisable to a modern eye, and it is clear that we are dealing with indirect memories at best. It is the lost link with the ancient past which is responsible for this, and which leaves us hints and impressions rather than history. These are only the faint echoes of the old Pharaonic world. For anything more, something like the Rosetta Stone would be needed, and this was still keeping its silence.

When we turn to western Europe, the silence is even deeper. Here the problem goes back to the image that Egypt had acquired as being the home of esoteric knowledge. Much of this misconception can be laid at the door of a man named Horapollo, an Egyptian priest who wrote a manual of hieroglyphs, perhaps as late as the fifth century AD. The book was translated into Greek, and this is how it has come down to us. Horapollo's work is a typical false signpost: the information on it may be correct, but it points us in completely the wrong way. Horapollo informs us, for example, that the hieroglyph for a vulture was used to write the word for 'mother', because in nature there are no vultures which are male. Similarly, the sign for a hare can do duty for the word 'open', because this animal never closes its eyes. He was right about the meaning of these hieroglyphs, and he probably had access to good information, but he was determined to show that the Egyptians fashioned their entire writing system on a series of allegories and rarefied meditations about the universe. The message is that this nation of philosophers and religious visionaries codified their profoundest insights into the symbols on their obelisks and temples. This idea, which chimed in with much of the thinking about Egypt in late antiquity, was to lead students of hieroglyphs down a wrong road which stretched ahead for more than fifteen centuries. Even for the Romans, Egypt had been the home of the exotic, depicted as such in mosaics and featuring as the scene of fictional romances and stories of the macabre. The Egyptians were clearly not as other men. Their thoughts were never mundane, and the many signs in the writings which they had left behind them could never be like the workaday alphabets of Greek or Latin, Hebrew or Arabic.

Throughout the European Middle Ages, this notion of 'the wisdom of the Egyptians' held the stage. In the Renaissance, it was the only act on that stage, and it was destined to become more and more histrionic. The typical figure in this development of the drama is a German Jesuit named Athanasius Kircher (1602–80). Kircher was a true polymath, steeped in knowledge of the Bible and classical philosophy, particularly the mystically inclined Neoplatonism, which had had such an influence on Horapollo and his contemporaries. He knew Hebrew, and made contributions to linguistic theory, realising, for example, that Coptic must be descended from the language of the Pharaohs. He made a start on what would now be called comparative religion, studying what he could of Indian and Chinese beliefs, since he suspected that divine inspiration could be present there as well. He lowered himself into Vesuvius out of curiosity about volcanoes, and extended the scope of mechanical organs for use in churches. Mysteries fascinated him, and he worked for a while on the Voynich manuscript, an illustrated manual of strange plants and astronomical lore, accompanied by a script or scripts which even now resist our understanding. An interest in all things Egyptian, and particularly Egyptian religion, was therefore inevitable in such an inquisitive man. His great work, *Oedipus Aegyptiacus*, was published in four volumes between 1652 and 1654.

As a result of the greater part of a lifetime's study, Kircher felt able to decipher the inscriptions on one of the Egyptian obelisks which were to be found in Rome. According to him, this text opens as follows:

> *Hemphta the supreme spirit and archetype infuses its virtues and gifts in the soul of the sidereal world … whence comes the vital motion in the material and elemental world, and an abundance of all things and variety of species arises from the fruitfulness of the Osirian bowl, in which, drawn by some marvellous sympathy, it flows ceaselessly, strong in power hidden in its two-faced self.*

The inscription is now recognised as the name and official titles of Pharaoh Apries, the Hophra of the Bible, who reigned from 589 to 570 BC.

5. The obelisk in the Piazza di Spagna, Rome, as recorded in Athanasius Kircher's *Oedipus Aegyptiacus* (1652–4).

It is easy to laugh at Kircher, particularly when we discover that the publisher of his Egyptological tome was a man named Johannes Kinckius. But Kircher is not a ridiculous figure. He was one of the finest minds of the Counter-Reformation, and it would be naïve for us to imagine that we are superior, and that all our theorisings will look sane in a few hundred years' time. What was lacking for Kircher was what we would now sum up as the right conceptual framework: the idea that Egyptian hieroglyphs were a rational system which could convey mundane ideas such as numbers, dates, shopping lists and the length of Cleopatra's nose. Kircher had no such framework, because he had no Rosetta Stone to fix that framework for him. All he could do was reshuffle the immense knowledge he had acquired, in a form of endless patience rather than a partnership game. As a result, Kircher's work on hieroglyphs can only tell us a lot about Kircher, and little about ancient Egypt.

For a reaction to this sort of thing we must turn to Anglo-Saxon pragmatism and the Enlightenment. Edward Stillingfleete, a clergyman who was to become Bishop of Worcester, published a book in 1662 which was intended to counter atheism. This led him to study what was known of religion outside the Bible. Egypt, like other lands mentioned in the Bible, had been a colony founded by one of the sons of Noah after the Flood. Colonies, he decided, were prone to fantasising about their origins, and little accuracy of thought could be expected of them. He was particularly struck by a hieroglyphic inscription at Thebes which was quoted by the Church Father Clement of Alexandria as meaning 'God hates presumption.' If this was the height of the Egyptians' contribution to religious thought, the down-to-earth Stillingfleete concluded that 'all these hieroglyphics put together will make but one good one, and that will stand for *labour lost'*. This may not be the birth of scientific Egyptology, but it comes as a welcome gust of fresh air.

A new approach was slowly coming into being. William Warburton (1698–1779), another Anglican clergyman, who went on to be Bishop of Gloucester, turned to the origins of writing as part of an attempt to detect the hand of divine providence in history. Writing, he argued, began with the use of pictures. These were extended figuratively to ideas which could be derived by extension: for example, an eye could be used to represent divine omniscience. In the final stage, arbitrary choices had to be made to produce signs like the alphabetic ones which we know. Warburton also came to the conclusion that the inscriptions on the walls of Egyptian temples must have recorded historical achievements as well as religious sentiments, since this is what Roman historians said they did, and Egypt was presumably a rational society with a history like any other. These are striking advances, and Jean-François Champollion was to pay Warburton the tribute of saying that he was the only one of his predecessors who treated Egyptian writing sensibly.

Another figure who moved along the same lines was the Danish scholar Georg Zoëga (1755–1809). Like Athanasius Kircher, he was an intellectual from the north who migrated to Rome, where he could work surrounded by hieroglyphs. Zoëga followed Warburton in his belief that there was no reason to think that the Egyptians were different from other men. Their writing, too, was rational, and, if other scripts were anything to go by, it will have contained phonetic elements as well as symbols. He began counting the individual signs, a step on which all successful decipherments are based. He tried to read between the lines of Horapollo to show how phonetics, derived from Coptic, could have lain behind some of the explanations given in that book. He also argued, astutely, that the elongated ovals known as cartouches which appeared on many objects from Egypt contained the names of individual Pharaohs. He was on the right lines, though sometimes held back by the academic's virtuous fault of considering every possibility equally rather than taking risks. The preface to his great work on Egyptology, *De origine et usu obeliscorum* ('Obelisks: Their Origin and Purpose'), reminds us of a slightly hesitant Moses, who was permitted a sight of the promised land but was never to set foot in it:

> *Further goals I have thought best left to posterity. When Egypt is better known to scholars, and when the numerous ancient remains still to be seen there have been accurately explored and published, it will perhaps be possible to learn to read the hieroglyphs and more intimately to understand the meaning of the Egyptian monuments.*

This was published in 1797. The following year, a new world would come into being.

2

THE POT AND THE KETTLE

If I was King of England, I would make you the most noble, puissant Duke Nelson, Marquis Nile, Earl Alexandria, Viscount Pyramid, Baron Crocodile and Prince Victory that posterity might have you in all forms.

Emma Hamilton, letter to Horatio Nelson, 26 October 1798

The first world war began in 1793 and lasted until the Battle of Waterloo in 1815. It was fought between the superpowers of the day. One of these, France, had helped to deprive the hated British of their control over much of North America. Now it was embarking on more than two decades of revolutionary fervour and European conquest. Britain became the paymaster, and then increasingly a combatant, in the coalition which succeeded in bringing French ambitions down. One of the consequences was the rise of British sea power to global supremacy, a state of affairs which was to continue for most of the next century. (Napoleon himself likened the conflict between Britain and France to a whale fighting an elephant.) There was scarcely a continent which was not dragged into the hostilities, and the political maps of Europe, the Americas and parts of Asia all needed to be redrawn as a result of the conflict. The immense energies released by the revolution in France, and the allied invasion which followed it, were first channelled by Napoleon and then usurped by him. This may have been the first occasion in modern history when a left-wing political movement found itself hijacked by a despot. It was not to be the last.

In May 1798 the French fleet of 400 vessels set out from Toulon, with orders to make for an undisclosed destination. Napoleon needed to strike a blow at the British, who had the annoying habit of remaining uninvaded on the other side of the Channel 35 kilometres away. He toyed with the idea of taking out Australia, but this would have been a symbolic gesture rather than a strategic one. India was the real prize, but a full-scale invasion would have been impractical in the midst of all-out war in Europe. However, if Egypt were to fall to French arms, the links between Britain and its growing Indian empire would be severed. The French had also nursed dreams of turning Egypt into a colony, dreams which had existed on and off since the days of St Louis and the Crusades, and the conquest of Egypt could lead to Syria and Jerusalem. Then there were the wonders of Egypt's exotic present, combined with its even more exotic and monumental past. As a result, the French fleet was accompanied by some 150 savants, experts in most of the known sciences, including astronomy, mathematics, agriculture and even musical notation, with the aim of recording everything they set their eyes on and everything they heard. This culture-added aspect of Napoleon's invasion force is unique in history.

At the beginning of July Napoleon and his troops landed in Egypt, glad to be rid of constant seasickness. Napoleon announced that he was a Muslim (he was always an opportunist), and that he had come to liberate the country from the

Mamelukes, a cabal of former slaves who had been ruling, or misruling, Egypt for several centuries. 'That gang of slaves,' ran part of the French proclamation, 'purchased in Georgia and the Caucasus, has held tyrannical sway over the most beautiful region on earth.' The Mamelukes disagreed with this. Later the same July there took place the celebrated Battle of the Pyramids, just outside Cairo. Napoleon made his famous speech, pointing to the majestic monuments and telling his soldiers that 4,000 years of history were looking down on them. (Here he underestimated the age of the Pyramids a little, but it was not a bad guess.) At first the Mamelukes put up effective resistance, but the training and superior arms of the French troops soon drove many of them into the Nile. This stage of the battle is the subject of the well-known panorama by Louis Lejeune, now in Versailles. The plunder, which included gold pieces as well as arms, must have been among the greatest of any known battle. Cairo was taken, the first printing press in the Arab world was installed to issue the new government's declarations, and the 150 savants got down to their research.

On its way to Egypt, the French fleet had been tracked up and down the Mediterranean by Admiral Nelson. At one point, not far from Crete, the two navies had passed each other in thick fog, and only an order to the French sailors to keep absolute silence enabled them to avoid being detected. Nelson caught up with the enemy at the end of July, while they were moored in Aboukir Bay, east of Alexandria. The Battle of the Nile, as this engagement is usually named, took place after dark on 1 August. It was fought against all the rules of the textbooks and the laws of common sense, being staged at night and in waters for which there were no charts, and

6. A detail from *The Battle of the Pyramids* by Louis-François Lejeune (1808).

it is Nelson's most brilliant victory. The British manoeuvred between the French ships and the shore, and attacked them from both sides. At ten o'clock the French flagship, *L'Orient*, exploded, and the noise could be heard 24 kilometres away. The British lost 218 men, the French some 1,700, including their brave admiral. His equally heroic son perished at his post, and was turned into the boy who 'stood on the burning deck whence all but he had fled', in the once-celebrated poem 'Casabianca', by Felicia Dorothea Hemans. Napoleon had no fleet left, and Nelson himself commented, 'Victory is not a name strong enough for such a scene.'

This battle struck a major blow to French ambitions, but the British were unable to prevent Napoleon sneaking out of the country twice, once to Syria and back, and finally to home, all under the noses of their blockading ships. Napoleon offloaded the command of the Army of Egypt on to his general, Jean-Baptiste Kléber (1753–1800). The son of a stonemason, Kléber had been appointed a division commander for the Egyptian expedition and was wounded during the landing at Alexandria. In spite of the trust placed in him, Napoleon's protégé was not impressed by this gesture, and he lost no time in opening negotiations with the Turks, the nominal rulers of the country. This led to frantic diplomacy involving most of the actors in this complicated drama, with the British trying to prevent the French surrendering to the Turks and not to them.

Meanwhile, Kléber had won an impressive victory against the Turkish forces, and it was becoming clear to the British that sinking the French fleet was not enough. If the whale was to succeed in driving out the elephant, there would need to be a landing in the country as well. It was not until the spring of 1801 that this took place, by which time Kléber had been assassinated. Aboukir Bay was again the setting for a British fleet, this time commanded by a Scot, Sir Ralph Abercromby. Nearby Alexandria was thinly defended and could have been taken with ease, but Abercromby did not realize this, and he shortly afterwards died as a result of a French counter-attack. Instead, the British resorted to breaching the natural causeway between the lakes which lay on either side of the city. This cut the French off from reinforcements, but the action was essentially a crime against the environment, not to mention the cultural heritage of one of the greatest cities of the ancient world. It was during this operation that the British succeeded in capturing the town of Rosetta, together with its fort.

The new British commander made for Cairo, taking thirty-seven days for a journey that Napoleon had done in eleven. The French refused to surrender: far from it, they let off a cannonade upon hearing a rumour that they had captured Ireland. The British, however, were soon joined by a considerable Mameluke force. Major reinforcements from India had also landed on the Red Sea coast (June 1801). The French forces, realising the impossibility of holding out, suffering from disease, and no doubt homesick for the attractions of their native land, agreed to evacuate Egypt. Napoleon's occupation of the country was at an end. His extravagant Sèvres dinner service with Egyptian themes, which was designed as a divorce gift to his empress Josephine, was eventually to be given to the Duke of Wellington, and is now in London, not far from the Rosetta Stone.

The French savants, on the other hand, had not been defeated, and they went on to triumph. One of the expedition,

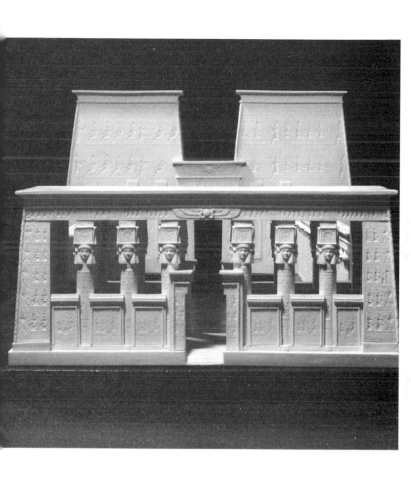

7. The temple of Dendera in Upper Egypt is the inspiration for the centrepiece of the Egyptian dinner service in Sèvres porcelain, commissioned for Napoleon (1810–12).

Vivant Denon (1747–1825), returned swiftly to France and published an illustrated account, *Voyage dans la basse et la haute Égypte* ('Travels in Lower and Upper Egypt'), which became a sensation when it appeared in 1802. More was to follow. Between the years 1809 and 1828 volume after volume came out, containing the results of the expedition's researches. Collectively, these volumes (nine of text and eleven of illustrations) are known as the *Description de l'Égypte*. The travelling experts studied the agriculture of Egypt and how it could be modernised, they established what nowadays would be called the anthropology of the country, and they published details of almost every temple, wall and hieroglyph that they could find, including the texts on the Rosetta Stone. Many of their illustrations show monuments that were destroyed later in the nineteenth century. In some cases, the French publication is the only record we will ever have. Since the savants could not read hieroglyphs, their recording of individual signs is often approximate, and some of the composite views of ancient Egypt would look more at home in an over-the-top performance of *The Magic Flute*. But the achievement of the French scholars, and their inspired editors, in producing the *Description* would be remarkable in any circumstances, and in reality their circumstances were difficult in the extreme.

The savants' monument is Egyptology's first database, and one of its most glamorous. France may have been denied political control over Egypt, but it was determined to hold on to cultural control. This is one of the reasons for the intense importance attached to the publication of the *Description de l'Égypte* in a country which had lost the global war. The desire for hieroglyphs to remain French was to manifest itself in other ways as well.

8. The Colossi of Memnon of Thebes, as recorded in the pages of the
Description de l'Egypte.

The French forces had taken steps to protect the Egyptian coast against the British navy, and at Rosetta, which was the first sizeable town to the east of Alexandria, they reconstructed the citadel, which they knew as Fort St Julien. There, in the middle of July 1799, an officer of engineers named Pierre François-Xavier Bouchard found the trilingual piece of granite that is the subject of this book. It was taken to the tent of General Menou, who had succeeded Kléber, and it was soon realised that the Greek decree at the bottom of the stone stated clearly that the Egyptian registers were versions of the same text. It looked as if the stone was a true key: decipherment, after all, can only go from the known to the unknown, and in this equation it was the Greek language that was the known. Could the lines of the Greek text take us into the hieroglyphic unknown?

Fort St Julien was not thought to be the right home for such an important piece of antiquity, and it was moved to Cairo, to the savants' headquarters at the Institut d'Égypte. Whether Napoleon saw it there is not recorded. At the Institut copies were made, which eventually found their way to several European countries, including ones, like England, with which the French were still at war. But the stone was not to remain in Cairo for long. It was becoming clear that the French presence in Egypt was drawing to an end and the capital was untenable. General Menou still held out in Alexandria, however, and the stone was obliged to retrace its journey across the Delta, to rejoin him in his tent.

Menou asked for an armistice on 26 August. Under the terms of this, all antiquities in the possession of the French were to be considered public property, subject to the disposal of the victorious generals. This was a euphemism for 'forfeit to the British'. Menou then declared that the French delegation had in their possession a total of two sarcophagi, a reply which everybody knew was somewhat economical with the truth. What about the stone? That, said Menou, happened to be his own personal property, something that could not possibly fall under the terms of any armistice; the same, he added, was true of all the other more attractive pieces that were lying around the place. The fact that the stone was at that moment hidden under mats in his warehouse was presumably to protect it from the fierce sunlight.

The French pot and the English kettle now started to point to each other's moral melanism. General Hutchinson, Menou's opposite number, explained to his opponent that in demanding these antiquities he was only following the example of the French themselves, who had looted the *Apollo Belvedere* and the *Laocoön* and other things from Rome, and were notorious for appropriating other people's treasures. Menou retorted that the English had long set an example to the entire universe of laying their greedy hands on anything that suited them. Thus began a dispute about the ownership of the past which is still with us.

Menou was a soldier and he knew when he was beaten. But the savants were academics and they resorted to the tricks that academics know: historical analogy and histrionic outrage. Rather than let this barbarous act of cultural vandalism go unreviewed, protested one of their number, these treasures should be scattered to the sands of the Libyan desert or cast into the depths of the sea. Another, Geoffroy St Hilaire, postured that the correct course was to burn these irreplaceable treasures: the library at Alexandria had gone up in flames in antiquity, and now the British would have the dubious pleasure of knowing that they had burned a second one. An eyewitness described the scene as follows:

> We remained near the outside of the tent; and soon heard the French General's voice elevated as usual, and in strong terms of indignation remonstrating against the injustice of the demands made upon him. The words 'Jamais on n'a pillé le monde' [Never has the world been so looted!] diverted us highly, as coming from a leader of plunder and devastation …

In its first two millennia the stone had been content with ancient Egyptian and Greek, and it probably never needed to learn Arabic. But in the few months of its new life it would have done well to acquire a working knowledge of English and French, in order to listen in on the controversy it was arousing. Soon it would also hear that it was on its way to England.

The person to whom the task of transporting the Rosetta Stone was entrusted was Sir Tomkyns Hilgrove Turner, known to his family as Hilgrove, and the name of the ship in which it was taken to England was *L'Égyptienne*. As the name indicates, this was a French frigate (French ships of this size were often faster than their British counterparts), and it had been captured in Alexandria harbour. If the stone has a sense of humour, as the history surrounding it suggests it does, it would have appreciated this irony.

The stone arrived at Portsmouth in February 1802, and reached London at Deptford, where its first experience of its new terra firma was in the Customs House. The existence of the stone, and the fact that it was on its way to London, had been announced to the public in the *Gentleman's Magazine* for 1801, but there are no accounts of cheering crowds on the quaysides welcoming it to its new home. The stone's fame was to come later. At first it was kept in the offices of the Society of Antiquaries of London, where it could be inspected by the academically curious, but it belonged to the entire nation, and a few months later it was transferred to the British Museum, together with the other antiquities which were supposed to be sacrificed on the altar of academic indignation. It now bore two extra inscriptions: 'Captured in Egypt by the British Army 1801' and 'Presented by King George III'. These sentiments are still visible, painted on both sides of the stone, but the British Museum has had the decency to let them fade. The antiquities in London were tokens of victory and their physical ownership was settled. But was the science that they represented going to be acquired from the French in the same way? Who were to be the true masters of Egyptology, the British or the French?

THE MAN OF SCIENCE

Then felt I like some watcher of the skies
When a new planet swims into his ken,
Or like stout Cortez when with eagle eyes
He stared at the Pacific – and all his men
Look'd at each other with a wild surmise –
Silent, upon a peak in Darien.

John Keats, 'On First Looking into Chapman's Homer' (1816)

Thomas Young was born at Milverton, in Somerset, on 16 June 1773, and he died on 10 May 1829, at the age of fifty-five. This makes him almost an exact contemporary of Ludwig van Beethoven (1770–1827), whose *Pathétique* sonata was first published in the year that the Rosetta Stone was discovered. Beethoven is perhaps the most important representative of this period of European revolution, but this can only be a relative estimate, since it was an age that produced one genius after another. Europe and America were in turmoil for much of these years, but out of this turmoil came a time when all was new and all was wonder. New planets were sailing into men's view, and men of science were there to record them and give them names.

Young was educated in Edinburgh, the capital of a country

whose cultural ties have often been with the Continent as much as with England. He then studied at Göttingen, a seat of learning which had strong links with Hanoverian Britain. The latter university in particular held a fond place in his memory. Young's European connections were greatly valued in his own country; and they were useful in later life, when he became foreign secretary of the Royal Society. The training he received in Germany was followed by more study, this time at Emmanuel College, Cambridge. Young's family was not poor, since his father was a minor banker as well as a mercer, but there were ten children to support, and Young's position at his various places of study must have been anomalous. He was a scholar of limited means who needed to earn his place in society, as opposed to the sons of the aristocracy, who were mainly there to amuse themselves. This was certainly true at Cambridge. Perhaps it was in the spirit of amusement that Young's contemporaries there, noting his intense curiosity about the natural world, gave him the nickname 'Phaenomenon Young'. Although Young came to Cambridge at the late age of twenty-three, when he was already a Fellow of the Royal Society, there is a resemblance to another man of science, Isaac Newton, who had been an undergraduate in the same university more than a century before. Newton had earned his keep while a student as a scholarship boy who did menial tasks and waited upon his richer contemporaries. Young was not as poor as this, but social distinctions of a similar sort remained strong, and they must have been felt by a man from the provinces with a Nonconformist background. This is not the only point of comparison between the two men. Young left Cambridge in the spring of 1799 for London, where he probably felt more at home.

The death of a wealthy great-uncle soon changed Young's fortunes, and made sure that he felt at home in London. Nominally Young earned his living as a doctor of medicine, but he no longer needed to support himself this way. For some of the time he was based at Worthing, on the south coast, but he also had a practice in the capital, where a blue plaque on the wall of 48 Welbeck Street records the fact that Thomas Young, man of science, lived at that address. During his career he was able to find the time for a series of scientific discoveries, any one of which would have been enough to make his reputation. He revolutionised the entire subject of mechanics, and added to this the wave theory of light, which lies at the root of modern optics and much else. There is even a demonstration of the nature of light itself which goes under the terse name of Young's experiment. This was presumably not the only experiment which Young did, but the opticians are keen to have his name on it. Here his work proved controversial, especially in his own country, where any departure from the work of Isaac Newton was thought to be heresy. But the heresy, in this case, turned out to be the truth.

In anatomy, Young's work on the human eye was revolutionary, and anyone who suffers from astigmatism or several other defects of vision has reason to be grateful to him. He identified the mechanism by which the eye perceives colours, and even managed to explain the iridescent nature of soap bubbles, a phenomenon which has fascinated many generations of schoolchildren. He produced a machine for measuring blood corpuscles. He also worked on acoustics, and designed a primitive light bulb. In the realm of physics, he came up with Young's modulus, which is something to do with elasticity in solid materials. Modern engineers say that it is concerned with the relationship between strain and stress, and they would be lost without it. He also coined the scientific use of the term 'energy', which lies at the heart of dynamics and quantum theory. Much of his work was so original that it bypassed his contemporaries. The physiologist Hermann von Helmholtz, for example, writing in 1852, describes a single one of Young's achievements as follows:

> *The theory of colours, with all these marvellous and complicated relations, was a riddle which Goethe in vain attempted to solve; nor were we physicists and physiologists any more successful. I include myself among the number; for I long toiled at the task, without getting any nearer my object, until I at last discovered that a wonderfully simple solution had been discovered at the beginning of this [nineteenth] century, and had been in print for any one to read who chose. This solution was found and published by the same Thomas Young who first showed the right method of arriving at the interpretations of Egyptian hieroglyphics. He was one of the most acute men who ever lived, but had the misfortune to be too far in advance of his contemporaries. They looked on him with astonishment, but could not follow his bold speculations, and thus a mass of his most important thoughts remained buried and forgotten in the* Transactions of the Royal Society *until a later generation by slow degrees arrived at the rediscovery of his discoveries, and came to appreciate the force of his arguments and the accuracy of his conclusions.*

This may be a bit romantic, but it is a moving tribute from one man of science to another. As if this were not enough, Young made notable contributions to navigation and the problem of determining longitude at sea, a theme which has been the surprising subject of a runaway best-seller. Young had a blind spot about astronomy, perhaps thinking it too far out of this world, but longitude was practical and something different. He was also a precocious learner of languages, and he is the inventor of the term Indo-European, as applied to the linguistic family discovered in the 1780s by Sir William Jones. (This family contains not only English and French, the languages of the Napoleonic rivals, but also most of the rest of the European languages, as well as Persian and many of the dialects of modern India.) Young went on to review about 400 languages for the *Encyclopaedia Britannica*, in addition to the articles he wrote for the same publication on natural science. While Francis Bacon may claim to be the last man in England to possess universal knowledge, Thomas Young's *Lectures in Natural Philosophy* (1807) come astonishingly near to it, at least in the realm of the physical sciences. I once gave a general talk on Young to a group of businessmen, and someone asked at the end whether this was the Thomas Young who invented Young's principles of life insurance. I said that I doubted it; I was of course wrong.

In this ceaseless activity we can detect something of Young's upbringing as a Quaker, a sect which emphasises moral rectitude, lack of ritual and simplicity of manners. As a teenager, he refused to take sugar on the grounds that it was associated with the slave trade. Much of his work is characterised by a feeling that all truths, however complex, could be expressed in terms that were essentially simple, and by an unremitting belief in the importance of hard work. On his deathbed he continued to work on his Egyptian dictionary, holding a pencil, since he could no longer use a pen. Even at

9. The polymath genius Thomas Young.

this point he remarked that he hoped to live to see the work finished; if not, then at least he would never have spent an idle day.

Young was interested in anything at the frontier of knowledge, and it was natural that he should turn to the question of ancient Egypt and its mysterious writing. He was introduced to the subject in 1814, when he was shown a demotic papyrus which had newly arrived from Thebes, and this led him on to a study of the middle section of the Rosetta Stone, the one which contained the demotic text. Even at this stage he was able to grasp that the demotic script was derived from hieroglyphs, and, since demotic appeared to contain phonetic elements as well as other signs and groups of signs which were more problematic, there was a chance that the hieroglyphic text of the stone would also turn out to be a complex script. Until then, the prevailing view was still the one that went back to Horapollo: the hieroglyphic system was either a series of recondite symbols or a script like Chinese which was bound to resist decipherment by virtue of its impenetrability. At the same time Young was aware of the possibility that the clue to the ancient language lay in Coptic, and he turned to learning this as well.

As we have seen in Chapter 1, William Warburton and Georg Zoëga had made inroads into the idea that Egyptian writing contained the secrets of a highly esoteric priestly class, obsessed with theological speculation and the mysteries of a divinely ordained cosmos. But this too could turn out to be a fantasy, even if the Greek text of the stone was implying that the Egyptian sections were equally factual. There remained the possibility that Egyptian writing was scarcely a rational system at all, if by this term is meant something with phonetic sounds, predictable grammar and an ability to convey ephemera such as the price of donkeys. According to the traditional view, hieroglyphs were ethereal or they were nothing.

However, as Louis Pasteur remarked, success in science comes only to the mind which is prepared, and Young was such a mind. He proceeded with great speed to identify words and phrases in the demotic version with similar expressions in the Greek equivalent, and while this method left room for mistakes, it was essentially the correct approach, and one which cumulatively was bound to lead to promising results. Young's attraction to demotic rather than to the hieroglyphs is explained partly by the fact that the demotic version on the stone is far more complete, but also by the likelihood that it was the demotic register which contained a natural language and a rational script with which to write it. Hieroglyphs may have reminded Young of astronomy, whereas demotic looked more like practical navigation. The scientist in Young was at home with the demotic script, in the way that was not the case with the more arty hieroglyphs. It is also possible that his Quaker upbringing prejudiced him in its favour; there were less likely to be arcane and Jesuitical messages in demotic.

All this meant that Young chose to tackle Egyptian from the more difficult end, since the demotic script is a form of shorthand, and far more abstract than its hieroglyphic parent. Whatever the reason for his choice, Young's work on the demotic script has not been fully appreciated. In 1819 he published in the *Encyclopaedia Britannica* an article which we can call state of the art, in which he offered equivalents for 218 demotic words, as well as 200 hieroglyphic groups. This article was later described by a French Egyptologist, François

Chabas, as follows: '*Cette idée fut, dans la réalité,* le Fiat Lux *de la Science*' ('This idea was, in effect, the *Let there be Light* of Egyptology').

Even more remarkable is Young's posthumous work, *Rudiments of an Egyptian Dictionary in the Ancient Enchorial Character* (1831), which contains his translation of an entire demotic contract as well as considerable portions of the Rosetta text. It also contains a transcription of several words and phrases into Coptic. A promising start to the study of demotic had been made by the Swedish diplomat Johan David Åkerblad, but he was not to follow this up. Young, on the other hand, was the first person since the end of the Roman Empire to be able to make sense of a demotic text, and, in spite of a fair proportion of incorrect guesses, he probably deserves to be known as the decipherer of demotic.

Young's contribution to hieroglyphs is more patchy and controversial. This was essentially confined to the period 1814–17, when he was already in his mid-forties. Most of his work on this script seems to have been done in the romantic setting of Worthing, during summer breaks from the capital. He began by looking at some papyrus fragments which had been brought back by a wealthy collector, but from these he soon progressed to the text on the stone itself. This led him to start a correspondence with one of the leading orientalists of the day, the French scholar Silvestre de Sacy, who encouraged him in his research, in spite of the politics which divided their countries. Young was aware that Åkerblad had published a short study on the text of the stone, suggesting that an alphabetic scheme might lie behind the hieroglyphics in some way. Could this idea be taken further?

The notion was gaining ground that the oval frames, or

cartouches, which appeared in more and more of the inscriptions being discovered contained the names of kings, and a study of the Greek text of the stone strongly suggested that this was the case, since royal names could be seen here in more or less the same places as the cartouches in the Egyptian. The name of the Pharaoh on the stone was Ptolemy Epiphanes, the fifth king in the dynasty to bear that name, but the text also contained the name of an earlier queen, Berenice, and this name was also found in Young's copy of another inscription, this time from Karnak. Young went on to identify alphabetic signs in both names, which was a considerable step forward, given that the cartouches also contained elaborate epithets. Not all of his identifications are correct, but the method is right, and this is what was important.

Young's approach to the understanding of the stone went further than a few letters of an alphabet. As a consequence of his methodical training, he painstakingly analysed the text of the stone word for word, pointing to equivalences between groups of hieroglyphs and words or phrases in the Greek. This way he was able to isolate key words such as 'king' and 'Egypt', together with the conjunction 'and'. He also succeeded in making sense of the numerical system used in hieroglyphic. This may seem elementary to us, but in reality it was a breakthrough of a high order. Uncharacteristically, Young then overreached himself, coming up with an entire 'translation' of the Egyptian text which ran away with itself. This was a bad lapse, but once again it is his method which is the real step forward.

In February 1818 Young wrote a letter to the collector and connoisseur William Bankes, who was busy creating his country seat at Kingston Lacy in Dorset and was in the

10. The other key to Egypt: hieroglyphs on the obelisk at
Kingston Lacy, Dorset.

process of shipping an obelisk back from Egypt. In this letter Young gives thirty-six names or other words accompanied by their hieroglyphic equivalents. Almost all of these are correct. At this point, Young was ahead of any other scholar in his understanding of the Rosetta Stone. The summers in Worthing had not been idled away.

In spite of these promising starts, Young did not take his hieroglyphic work further, and the Bankes letter, together with the encyclopedia article of 1819, represents the peak of his achievement. He could not overcome his suspicion that the alphabetic elements that he had discovered were used only for foreign names and that the rest of the hieroglyphs could not be explained along those lines. All the same, his reluctance to extend his studies in Egyptology seems puzzling. It was noted by contemporaries, and the Italian Copticist Amedeo Peyron summoned up the courage to write to Young to say so. His letter, which cleverly combines Italian flattery with Latin incisiveness, is illuminating:

> You write that from time to time you will publish new material which will increase our knowledge of Egyptian matters. I am very glad to hear this, and I urge you to keep your word. For, as Champollion will witness, and other friends to whom I have mentioned your name, I have always felt, and so do many others, that you are a man of rare and superhuman genius with a quick and penetrating vision, and you have the power to surpass not only myself but all the philologists of Europe, so that there is universal regret that your versatility is so widely engaged in the sciences – medicine, astronomy, analysis, etc., etc. that you are unable to press on with your discoveries and bring them to that pitch of perfection which we have the right to expect from a man

of your conspicuous talents; for you are constantly being drawn from one science to another, you have to turn your attention from mathematics to Greek philosophy and from that to medicine etc. The result is that there are some mistakes in your books which you yourself might well have corrected.

This is a powerful letter. It underestimates Young's contribution to science, but it pinpoints his weaknesses as well as his strengths. It is possible that Peyron's tactful rebuke did strike home, and this may explain why Young continued to work on demotic. But Young did not return to hieroglyphics, and Peyron was right that other matters were claiming his attention.

There is certainly a deeper explanation at work. Young was a genius – even if an underrated one – but he was not what most of us would call an Egyptologist. Peyron was wrong to imagine that he was. The energy that drove Young took him in all directions: he was essentially a solver of problems, who would tackle a problem because it was a problem, until he achieved the decisive breakthrough. After that, he would move on to another mystery, often in an entirely different field. It was noted that he would never repeat an experiment if he could avoid it. This does not mean that he was superficial or had a butterfly mind; quite the reverse, his work is characterised by an almost unparalleled series of insights. But it remains true that Young's restlessness was both his strength and his weak point.

In reality, Young's interest in Egyptology seems to have deteriorated quite rapidly. In a letter to former school friend and one-time pupil Hudson Gurney, written as early as the beginning of 1816, he remarks, 'All the inscriptions on temples, and the generality of the manuscripts found with mummies, appear to relate to their ridiculous rites and ceremonies: I see nothing that looks like history.' Here perhaps we have the ritual-averse Quaker speaking. In 1817 Young proposed the creation of an Egyptian Society, which would publish all the known hieroglyphic inscriptions, 'and perhaps for employing some poor Italian or Maltese to scramble over Egypt in search of more'. Maybe he toyed with the idea of Champollion for such a menial role; at any rate, it is clear that he did not envisage it for himself. It is no surprise to discover that the proposed Egyptian Society did not last.

This lack of affinity with hieroglyphs makes Young's attachment to demotic, which spanned the last fifteen years of his life, all the more remarkable. The best description of his attitude to his work is contained in a letter Young himself wrote, again to Hudson Gurney. This was no dry-as-dust compiler of notebooks:

> *I like a deep and difficult investigation when I happen to have made it easy to myself if not to all others – and there is a spirit of gambling in this, whether as by the cast of a die, a calculation* à perte de vue *shall bring out a beautiful and simple result, or shall be wholly thrown away. Scientific investigations are a sort of warfare, carried on in the closet or on the couch against all one's contemporaries and predecessors; I have often gained a signal victory when I have been half asleep, but more frequently found, on being thoroughly awake, that the enemy had still the advantage of me when I thought I had him fast in a corner – and all this, you see, keeps me alive.*

Nelson would have approved of this, and so, ironically, would

Napoleon. In later years much of Young's Quakerism lapsed. He was received into the Church of England, but it may be that it was wrestling with the unknown that had become his true religion.

Champollion, who was seventeen years Young's junior, is rightly called the father of Egyptology, but even fathers need to be created, and this is where Young comes in: he can be seen as the spiritual father of Champollion's decipherment. He was not his teacher and he did not go out of his way to make things easy for him. He did not inspire Champollion's interest in his studies. What Young did, and perhaps no one else could have done, was to clear away the accumulated mis-understandings which were preventing the birth of a deci-pherment. One of the best tributes to his overall achievement is contained in an address to the Optical Society of America at the beginning of the 1920s by M. H. E. Tscherning:

> *If you take Young as the first man in the question of the theory of light, the name of the second man is Fresnel; in the question of the anomalies of refraction of the human eye, the name of the second man is Donders; in the question of colour senses, you can call the second man Clerk Maxwell, or Helmholtz; in the question of hieroglyphics the name of the second man is Champollion; in the question of terrestrial radiant heat the name of the second man is Wells, and I have not yet finished the list. For his own reputa-tion it would certainly have been better if Young had completely developed but one of his ideas. But for the advancement of science it was better that he did as he did.*

This does not do justice to Champollion, but there is an element of truth in what is being said here. Young's discoveries follow a regular pattern: once he had achieved them, it was essential for him to move on, leaving the subject that he had sketched in outline to be painted in full by others. In essence, his imagination was scientific and abstract; poetry, human society and human affairs had comparatively little interest for him, not because he held these things in contempt, but because they could not easily be expressed in formulae. He was convivial, and he is said to have been a good dancer and a competent musician, but his true life was that of an analyst, a thinker at the frontiers of science.

Keats, in the extract quoted at the beginning of this chapter, likened his reading of Homer to the discovery of a new planet. This is an apt analogy, although it may not have interested Young very much. Before the decipherment of the Rosetta Stone, the only cultural planets in the firmament of western man were Greece, Rome and the Bible. Ancient Egypt swam into view at the beginning of the romantic era (this is the subject's strength, and the source of much of its attraction, but it is also the cause of some of its problems). The ancients had known five physical planets in their own heavens, and it was not until 1781 that Uranus was discovered by William Herschel, a German resident in England. Young would have been a child of seven or eight at the time. The asteroid Ceres was discovered on 1 January 1801, and was nicknamed 'the new planet for the new century'. It may have been this that Keats had in mind when he wrote his poem.

There is a parallel between the decipherment of hieroglyphs and the discovery of the next planet, Neptune. Even though nobody had seen it, the position of this planet was calculated in England by John Adams, then an undergraduate student at Cambridge. His discovery was sent to the

Astronomer Royal in London but not followed up, in a combination of brilliant insight and poor application which seems peculiarly British. Meanwhile, Urbain Leverrier in Paris had made a similar calculation, and sent his results to Berlin. Berlin lost no time in pointing its telescope to the right part of the sky and Neptune was duly discovered in 1846, within what should have been the lifetime of Champollion. Nowadays both astronomers, the Englishman and the Frenchman, are given credit for the achievement. In the case of hieroglyphs, the position of Young does not equal that of his French colleague, but he is entitled to a place in Egyptology's roll of honour.

There is a postscript to this. When Galileo first looked at the heavens through his small telescope, he found, much to the annoyance of the Church, the moons of Jupiter. Night after night he drew them against the background of the stars, to show that they were rotating, and to prove that Aristotle's static universe could no longer be true. One of the stars in the background seemed to move a little, but Galileo ascribed this to a fault in his telescope, or in himself: moons and the five planets move, but stars do not. We now know that he was looking at Neptune, but it was not given to him to realise this. Whether we can call Galileo the discoverer of Neptune is a rarefied question, but one answer has to be that the Italian was the first to see the planet, but he cannot have discovered it, since he did not know what he was seeing. At the time, there was no conceptual framework for the idea that there could be other, invisible planets, and not even Galileo was able to transcend this. There was a similar lack of a framework when Athanasius Kircher tried to translate his obelisk in Rome. In scientific discovery, the conceptual framework is the all-important first step. It is knowing what you are looking at, and it is the equivalent of Cortez standing on his alleged peak in Darien. In Egyptology, that framework was the achievement of Thomas Young. Put simply, Young stripped away the mystery which had accumulated round Egyptian hieroglyphs and showed that they too obeyed rational rules. This is brought out in his epitaph in Westminster Abbey, which reads, in the distinctly florid language of the day:

> *Fellow and Foreign Secretary of the Royal Society, Member of the National Institute of France; a man alike eminent in almost every branch of human learning. Patient of unintermitted labour, endowed with the faculty of intuitive perception, who, bringing an equal mastery to the most abstruse investigations of letters and science, first established the undulatory theory of light, and first penetrated the obscurity which had veiled for ages the hieroglyphics of Egypt.*

Note that this epitaph does not use the word 'decipherer'. This is right, although the opposition which it makes between the theory of light and the darkness which veiled the Egyptian language is a neat one. But the point is clear. What Young did in hieroglyphs, while falling short of the name decipherment, shed indispensable light on what was to come. If Young had been born in any other European country there would be statues of him in public places. At the moment there is a plinth in Trafalgar Square which is still waiting for something permanent to go on top of it. Thomas Young, man of science, would be as good a candidate as any for this honour.

··

4

THE MAN OF ART

All that remains to add, to sum up, is that we Europeans are merely men of Lilliput, and no people ancient or modern has conceived of art or architecture on so sublime a scale, so broad, so grandiose, as did the Egyptians of old; they created like men a hundred feet high, and compared with this we at the very most are five foot eight.

Jean-François Champollion, letter from Egypt to his elder brother,
24 November 1828

Jean-François Champollion, the eventual decipherer of the Rosetta Stone, is invariably known as the father of Egyptology. This makes a good epitaph, but epitaphs are designed to bury their subject at the same time as extolling them. The living Champollion was a genius, but he was a singularly restless one. The combination of obscure origins and precocious brilliance left him in permanent rebellion, and his lifetime of scarcely forty-two years gave him much to rebel against. In his early years he was an unflinching supporter of Bonaparte, and he gave his support to social as well as political reform. His part in an uprising in Grenoble in 1821 led to him being charged with treason. If the Rosetta Stone had never been discovered, his essays, literary correspondence and poems would earn him a minor place within French literature. The contrasts between this mercurial figure and the mathematical Thomas Young could hardly be greater, but it was Egyptology in general, and the Rosetta Stone in particular, which brought them together. Champollion and Young were both remarkable intellects, but, more importantly to us, Champollion was a remarkable intellect who was also an Egyptologist. He breathed the subject from his boyhood. The combination of accuracy and empathy enabled him to race ahead of Young's work. His health was never good, but he could not abandon his mission. His commitment and love for his chosen profession are unique in the history of Egyptology, and there are times when it is tempting to think that Egyptology chose him, in order to be born.

Champollion himself was born in Figeac, a small town near Grenoble, on 23 December 1790. The family was not noticeably poor, at least in the earlier years when the father was able to run a small bookshop, but they were not exactly gentry either, and Champollion's mother never learned to read or write. Although there were five children in the family, the accounts of Jean-François' early years give the impression of a solitary character who hated the cold and spent many hours huddled by the fire. His health may already have been delicate and his primary education was patchy. He did not go to a regular school until he was seven, and even then his great intelligence and low boredom threshold made him an unruly pupil. He was soon taken out of school and given to a private tutor. Like Beethoven, Champollion had a mother who died young and a father who became an alcoholic. Also like Beethoven, but unlike Young, Champollion never mastered mathematics, and it was clear that he was not destined for the physical sciences.

One of the tales which survive from ancient Egypt, and which thanks to Champollion we can read, is known as *The Two Brothers*. At the beginning of this pastoral story, which dates from around 1300 BC, the two brothers live together on a farm, the younger helping his elder brother with the work. The greatest influence on the young Champollion was his elder brother, Jacques-Joseph, who was twelve years his senior and also his godfather. When Jacques-Joseph came of age he moved to Grenoble, and his younger brother joined him there in 1799, the year that the Rosetta Stone was discovered. Somehow Jacques-Joseph had developed a passionate interest in ancient Egypt, and the pair will have followed the news of Napoleon's expedition with intense anticipation, then gloom as the army capitulated. Grenoble offered the younger Champollion far greater opportunities for learning, and he began to master Hebrew, Arabic and Syriac. His study of Arabic led him to adopt the nickname Seghir ('Tiny'), which he used for the rest of his life in his correspondence with Jacques-Joseph. The direction of his talents was now clear. At one point the teenager fell ill with exhaustion. To help his convalescence, he asked his brother for a Chinese grammar: perhaps not a treatment a doctor, then or now, would recommend. On 1 September 1807, the sixteen-year-old announced to the Grenoble Society of Sciences and the Arts that he intended to decipher Egyptian and reconstruct the entire history of the Pharaohs. The dream and the man were already one and the same.

For much of its history France has been a centralised country, and it was inevitable that a youthful student with such a desire to learn would migrate to Paris. Here Champollion was to be taught by, among others, Silvestre de

Sacy, the scholar who a few years later was to correspond with Young about the inscriptions on the stone. Above all, this teacher introduced Champollion to Coptic, and the young man was soon studying the Coptic manuscripts in what was then termed the Bibliothèque Impériale.

Both brothers were passionate about the Rosetta Stone and the prospects for understanding it, and outsiders would have found them relentless about the subject. There was certainly a political dimension to this, as well as an intellectual one, since the stone had been discovered by the new France, and the ideals of the revolution were to spread enlightenment and do away with the old ignorance. For the first part of Champollion's career, Egyptology and politics were free to overlap. After Waterloo, however, much of this would have to be put on hold. While he was still only eighteen, Jean-François was awarded a joint post with his brother at the lycée of Grenoble. The position was poorly paid, and his tenure of it would turn out to be brief. For much of his life he was to exist on the edge of poverty, frequently dependent on his brother.

The combination of reduced means and indifferent health would blunt most people's optimism, but the astonishing thing about Champollion is his almost irrepressible energy and good spirits. This was the man who wrote, 'Enthusiasm, that is the only life.' Most of the time this almost manic idealism prevailed in him, although he could succumb to bouts of depression, and he may have suffered from what is increasingly referred to as a bipolar temperament. Whatever the truth, Champollion's seemingly unstoppable energy led him in 1814 to produce the first of his monumental works, *L'Égypte sous les Pharaons*, a two-volume encyclopedia containing

[59]

11. Before he was famous: a youthful Jean-François Champollion, painted *c*. 1810.

almost everything on the history, geography and chronology of ancient Egypt that the twenty-three-year-old had been able to gather from his unceasing research. The author sent a copy to London, mistakenly addressing it to the Royal Society rather than the Society of Antiquaries. This way, the books came into the hands of Thomas Young. The foreign secretary of the Royal Society now began his correspondence with his rival in France.

The second of Champollion's qualities was wit, and this could take an impish form. He wrote satirical songs about the royalist movement, which he had the sense to keep anonymous. When he was an established world authority on his chosen subject, he was still capable of sending the museum in Turin a letter from no less a person than King Ramesses II, giving the worthy curators of this great collection a series of instructions on how to look after the Pharaoh's monuments. It is reassuring to be reminded that this great ruler, the Ozymandias of Shelley's poem, was fluent in French as well as hieroglyphics. When it came to ancient Egypt, unlike contemporary France, Champollion had no problems about being a royalist. There is also a literary and somewhat bohemian side to Champollion which was absent from the sober Young. He composed limericks and plays, as well as tomes of Egyptology. It is not difficult to imagine Champollion getting drunk and coming out with indelicate but elegantly crafted verses. It is impossible to imagine Young doing this.

An impression of Champollion's enthusiasm and literary charm can be gained from his platonic but highly impassioned correspondence with a young Italian woman from Livorno, Angelica Palli, sometimes referred to as 'the Sappho of Piedmont'. Out of his enthusiasm for nicknames,

Champollion gave her the name Zelmire. These letters cover the period 1826–9, when his reputation as a decipherer was beginning to be made and when he had already been married for a decade. Egyptology and biblical chronology come into these letters, as is to be expected, but they also range over politics and literary criticism, including ways of improving the trashy popular novels which Champollion fears are flooding his native country. He quotes Benjamin Franklin to the effect that wealth is always a little more than one possesses, and constantly craves replies from his Zelmire, remarking that he is like a child where promises are concerned: never make one if you cannot keep it. There was a childlike, as opposed to childish, streak in Champollion which never left him.

We read Champollion's words, whether scientific or literary, with the vision of hindsight. We know the end of the story, and Champollion is the hero of it. We cannot fail to see him as the goody, and we forgive him his youthful excesses. Most of the time we even admire them. But the reality was that Champollion made enemies, and he made these enemies above all in his native country. It was jealous rivals who forced him out of his modest post in Grenoble, who did their best to delay the publication of *L'Égypte sous les Pharaons* and who spread doubts about his integrity. Not everyone trusted Champollion.

In the previous chapter, we saw that Thomas Young had been in touch with Champollion's teacher, Silvestre de Sacy. What we did not see was that de Sacy congratulated Young on being ahead of the work, and hoped for more, but he warned the Englishman that he should on no account trust his younger French colleague, who was capable of seizing any idea of Young's and claiming it as his own. In another letter, written in 1815, de Sacy describes his former pupil as 'prone to playing the role of a jackdaw in borrowed peacock's plumes'. Since Champollion was obsessed by anything to do with ancient Egypt, this warning was partly justified, and should not be dismissed purely as academic jealousy on the part of a former teacher. There was a similar motive behind the letter that Amedeo Peyron sent to Thomas Young which we read in the previous chapter. Peyron, who was greatly influenced by French culture, and who often used the form Amédée for his first name, nevertheless wanted the decisive break-through in the decipherment of Egyptian to come from an Englishman.

Some of this antipathy may have been personal, since the qualities of verve and commitment that we admire in Champollion may have seemed to contemporaries more like brashness. He was young, from the provinces, and in far too much of a hurry. But much of the resentment must have been political. The upheavals of the revolution and the Napoleonic struggles had left their mark on all the participating nations. Even Britain was undergoing strains, caused by half a century of war accompanied by rapid but uneven industri-alisation and economic growth. In Britain much of this was masked, especially as that country had emerged victorious at sea and highly influential on land. On the Continent things were more overt, and more polarised. This was particularly the case in France, which had lost the conflict, and was in danger of tearing itself in two. In such a situation, grudges, old scores and suspicions flourish. Champollion had been a sympathiser of Bonaparte, though he was never an uncriti-cal devotee, and on the day of Waterloo itself he published a pamphlet lampooning the Bourbon succession. This was to get him into real trouble. Contemporaries may well have felt, as they did about Beethoven, that there was something revolutionary about Champollion and his work.

This polarity between revolution and reaction had been a source of weakness in France even during the war. It was one reason why Napoleon, who did not trust the loyalty of some of his admirals, neglected the financing of his fleet and left it no match for Nelson's at Aboukir and Trafalgar. The political terms left and right are part of the legacy of the French Revolution (they derive from the seating arrangements in the assembly), and something of the same factionalism continues to this day. On a visit to Paris once I was entertained to an excellent lunch by a generous and likeable colleague. At one point he asked me why I was visiting Paris. I explained that it was, of course, to get to know him better, but I also wanted to meet another French Egyptologist, who was not present. A hush fell over the table; I had clearly said something very wrong. My hostess, seeing my embarrassment, said in something resembling a stage whisper, '*Le Professeur – est gauchiste.*' Champollion was a lefty too, in an age when revolution had been discredited, and this accounts for much of the hostility towards him. As Champollion began to go beyond anything which Young or anyone else was able to contribute to the study of hieroglyphs, this hostility could only grow.

One of Champollion's chief opponents was none less than the editor of the *Description de l'Égypte*, Edmé François Jomard, who took an instant dislike to him. He put every obstacle he could in the way of Champollion's advancement, undermining his credibility and sneering at this man, who had no money, for never having been to Egypt. The two clashed in particular over an ancient zodiac which was found carved on the roof of a chapel at Dendera in Upper Egypt. This was removed by the French expedition and transported to Paris at the beginning of 1822. The great Jomard had argued that this text was up to 15,000 years old, but Champollion was able to show that it was late by Egyptian standards, being a product of the Graeco-Roman period. This had an ironic result. The Roman Church, which had previously been suspicious of the provincial upstart who dabbled in ancient chronology, declared with relief that Champollion's conclusion vindicated the timescale implied in the Bible. Given that Champollion was essentially anti-clerical, he can only have felt that he was exchanging one set of headaches for another. His relations with the Church were later to turn reassuringly sour again.

All this time Champollion continued to work on the hieroglyphs. At this stage he had never visited England nor seen the Rosetta Stone, but he was able to work with copies which were available in Paris and were accurate enough for his purposes. The same at this stage of his life was true of the inscriptions found in Egypt, which could only be studied in the form of drawings or the occasional squeeze impressions. His acquaintance with the script constantly increased, but a vital thing was missing. Right up to the year 1821 he remained convinced that hieroglyphs were purely symbolic and he even published a book making this misleading point. It was quite some time before he was to become aware of Young's work and what it implied.

In the autumn of 1821 the obelisk which had been acquired by Young's friend William Bankes had arrived in England from the island of Philae, and the importance of it was not lost on Young: this text too was bilingual, being composed in Greek as well as hieroglyphic. This inscription mentioned the name Cleopatra, and it was not difficult to identify it in the hieroglyphs, since it contained up to six letters – *l*, *e*, *o*, *p*, *t* and *a* – which were also in the name Ptolemaios (Ptolemy), which featured repeatedly on the Rosetta Stone. Young wrote a note on this, and the note found its way to Champollion, in a marked copy sent to the author of *Voyage dans la basse et la haute Égypte*, Vivant Denon, at the Institut de France. The idea itself – as opposed to the use made of it – was not Champollion's, and by strict rights he should have acknowledged this.

Champollion has sometimes been accused of dishonesty here, by those who want to use hieroglyphs to reopen the Napoleonic Wars. This is the equivalent of accusing a vat of alcohol of lack of originality for bursting into flames when a lighted match is placed next to it. The Frenchman, whose instincts were pent up by years of frustration, must have realised in an instant where the true line of progress lay; in fact, all of his preparation in Egyptology must have been leading him to the point where he could see the truth of this. Now he knew what he was looking at. Within days, perhaps hours, he was beginning to go far beyond anything in Young's note. Any mention of Young at this point would only have been exploited by Champollion's enemies. In the longer run, he might well have reached the same conclusion unaided. There is no point in handing out blame: the history of scientific discovery is full of overlaps like this.

Champollion later claimed to have learned almost nothing from Young, and this has often been taken at face value. However, the odds are that there is more to it than this. In showing that Egyptian hieroglyphs were a system of writing that could be reduced to rules, Young was going over areas that had been tentatively explored by Warburton and Zoëga. Warburton, however, had been dead for forty years, and Zoëga for over a decade. They were safe. Young, on the other hand, was alive and was known to be one of the sharpest scientific minds in Europe. What else could he be planning? This was a serious threat, and one way of dealing with such a threat is denial.

On Friday 27 September 1822 the Académie des Inscriptions et Belles Lettres held one of its sessions in Paris. Among the names present were Thomas Young, who was there in his capacity of foreign secretary of the Royal Society, and the German geographer and ecologist Alexander von Humboldt. Papers at these sessions were always addressed to the presiding Fellow, and this was the classical scholar Bon-Joseph Dacier. The communication read out on that wet afternoon by Jean-François Champollion is forever known by the name *Lettre à Monsieur Dacier*. In this paper the younger French scholar outlined the hieroglyphic alphabet which he had succeeded in isolating from the Rosetta Stone and the Bankes obelisk, and stated his belief that such a phonetic system would turn out to be integral to hieroglyphic writing as a whole. As we have seen, a few of the phonetic values had already been anticipated by Young, but the second part of Champollion's claim – that earlier Egyptian would also turn out to contain phonetic elements – was more controversial, and the Englishman never succeeded in accepting it completely. Nevertheless, Young recorded his initial impressions of the occasion in a letter to one William Hamilton. This is not the diplomat and collector who is nowadays remembered as the husband cuckolded by Nelson, but his later namesake, who was responsible for getting the Rosetta Stone, and for that matter the Elgin Marbles, to the British Museum. Part of Young's letter is quoted in the British Museum catalogue of the Rosetta Stone exhibition, *Cracking Codes*:

> *I have found here, or rather recovered, Mr. Champollion, junior, who has been living these ten years on the Inscription of Rosetta, and who has lately been taking some steps in Egyptian literature, which really appear to be* gigantic. *It may be said that he found the key in England which has opened the gate for him, and it is often observed that* c'est le premier pas qui coûte; *but if he did borrow an English key, the lock was so dreadfully rusty, that no common arm would have strength enough to turn it; and, in a path so beset with thorns, and so encumbered with rubbish, not the first step only, but every step, is painfully laborious; especially such as are retrograde; and such steps will sometimes be necessary: but it is better to make a few false steps than to stand quite still. If Mr. Champollion's latest conjectures become confirmed by collateral evidence, which I dare say you will not think impossible, he will have the merit of setting the chronology of the later Egyptian monuments entirely at rest ... You will easily believe, that were I ever so much the victim of the bad passions, I should feel nothing but exaltation at Mr. Champollion's success: my life seems indeed to be lengthened by the accession of a junior coadjutor in my researches, and of a person too, who is so much more versed in the dialects of the Egyptian [i.e. Coptic] language than myself.*

The continuation is not quoted in *Cracking Codes*, but it is well worth adding:

> *I sincerely wish that his merits may be as highly appreciated by*

> *his countrymen and by their government as they ought: and I do not see how he can fail of being considered as possessing an undeniable claim to an early admission into any literary Society, that may have a place vacant for his reception. I have promised him every assistance in his researches that I can procure him in England, and I hope in return to obtain from him an early communication of all his future observations.*

Young may not have been the greatest stylist of English prose, and we may suspect that he is protesting a little too much. Some unease about Champollion does seem to be present beneath the measured generosity, and at one point he comes close to patronising him. But I cannot see in this letter the permanently embittered personality which has been suggested by some. As academic tributes towards rival colleagues who are still alive go, Young's comment on Champollion is one of the warmer ones. Of course, Young still represents himself as the mentor of his French colleague, and there is no doubt that he was tactless here, but this does not make it malicious.

Young and Champollion met several times in Paris and discussed not only Egyptology, but also a scheme for improving the education of the poor. This was an area where they could easily agree. Later the relations between the two scholars grew worse, mainly because Young himself lost most of his interest in the realm of hieroglyphics and took an increasingly sceptical view of what Champollion was trying to do. Champollion was on an unstoppable roll, as several of his contemporaries could attest, and the work of Young must have seemed increasingly irrelevant to him. In addition, the Frenchman was already the victim of the overwork that was to kill him. After 1825 Young's health in turn began to deteriorate. Gentlemanly correspondence tends to suffer in conditions such as these.

Young's attitude to Champollion, while mixed with some of the detachment commonly felt by Britons who visited post-Napoleonic France, mostly appears balanced and encouraging, and he specifically acquitted Champollion of any charge of plagiarism, although he did express regret that his own contribution had not been more freely acknowledged. Young, after all, had a secure place in the history of science, and any work that he achieved in Egyptology was merely a bonus to this. In some of his dealings with scientific colleagues, he could be as competitive as any academic; but with Champollion he could afford to be generous, and on the whole he was.

There is no doubt that Young denied the validity of much of Champollion's work, but he was not alone in this. He insisted on public acknowledgement of his own initial, and limited, discoveries, and this certainly rankled with Champollion. The Frenchman in him did not need to think twice before resenting a prior claim to his work from the other side of the Channel. The history of decipherment is an intensely disputed field, and one in which scholars frequently fall short of their best standards. There are plenty of cranky attempts at deciphering ancient inscriptions, and scepticism towards any new attempt is often a healthy reaction. Then there are the academic stakes, which are high, since a successful decipherment is the equivalent of intellectual immortality, and the thought that this could go to an upstart rival is a distinctly painful one. As if this were not enough, it is frustrating to see one's ideas coming to fruition in the hands of others, especially if they refuse to mention you or acknowledge where the ideas came from.

In the context of this sort of rivalry Young's opposition to Champollion's work seems mild, especially as he was not the only member of the world of learning to voice misgivings about what Champollion was trying to do. To see Thomas Young as the fallen angel of the Rosetta Stone, as is sometimes done, is to look through a jaundiced eye. To take an analogy from his scientific work, Young's theory of colour perception allows for three receptors in the human eye, one for red light, one for blue and one for green. In Young's scheme of things, there was no receptor set aside for yellow light. In 1828 he wrote a letter to a French colleague in which he says this of Champollion:

> *I am most ready to admit that the more I see of his researches the more I admire his ingenuity as well as his industry; and I must be eager to bear witness on every occasion to the kindness and liberality which he has shown me in either giving or procuring for me copies of everything that I have asked of him, out of the treasures entrusted to his care.*

During the many years when he was foreign secretary of the Royal Society, one of Young's duties was to write letters of congratulation to European scientists and scholars who had been elected to that body. Some of these were his rivals, and the academic world, then as now, was full of disputes and prior claims to knowledge. There is very little spite or jealousy in that correspondence. Compared with the paranoid feuds of Isaac Newton, Young was a model of diplomacy.

In the *Lettre à Monsieur Dacier*, Champollion kept back

much that he had already achieved, concentrating on the alphabetic scheme and resorting to generalities about the rest. He could not afford to reveal too much to his rivals, but in reality he was already moving fast. A successful decipherment begins slowly, but there comes a point when the movement of the snowball turns into an avalanche. Much of the work was done at Champollion's lodgings at 28 rue Mazarine, not far from the building where Molière made his first appearance on the stage. Two years later, in 1824, the results of his breakthrough were revealed, under the accurate but somewhat unsnappy title *Précis du système hiéroglyphique des anciens égyptiens*. Here he was able to sum up his understanding of the script that he had deciphered: 'Hieroglyphic writing is a complex system, a script at the same time figurative, symbolic and phonetic, in one and the same text, in one and the same sentence, and, if I may put it, almost in one and the same word.' He no longer had to make guesses; he was on the way home. By 1824 he had the confidence to admit that Young had been ahead of him in recognising the sound-values of some of the hieroglyphs. The issue no longer mattered, compared with what Champollion now knew.

The animosity that French colleagues directed against Champollion began gradually to fade, particularly as it was realised that the decipherment of hieroglyphs could be seen as a national honour. Napoleon had come and gone, and the monarchy had gone and returned. The France of the battlefield was a memory, and a memory tainted with defeat and recriminations. But the France of the mind could still be triumphant. The Rosetta Stone of geology may have found its way to London, but the Rosetta Stone of the intellect was to stand for ever in Paris. A fitting symbol of this reconciliation was when the classicist Jean Antoine Letronne, who had gone so far as to tell Thomas Young that Champollion was a charlatan, produced the formal publication of the Greek text on the Rosetta Stone and dedicated it to his former adversary.

In May 1826 Champollion was appointed to a curatorial post in the Louvre, an event which marks his acceptance into the junior levels of the French establishment. One of his first acts was to push through the purchase of a major collection which had been amassed by no less a person than the English consul in Egypt, Henry Salt. The British Museum had been hesitating over buying this, and this enabled the Louvre to stage its cross-Channel coup.

Another museum that was busy expanding was the one in Turin, which was at that time the capital of the kingdom of Savoy. Champollion had visited the Italian states and their collections in 1824–5, the first time he had left France, and he was able to pay a second visit shortly before he was appointed to the Louvre. His elder brother, who hyphenated the element Figeac to the family name, became the recipient of one ecstatic letter after another. The Turin museum in particular fascinated the decipherer. One way to expand the Savoy Egyptian holdings was to wait for Henry Salt to build up yet another collection. Salt was capable of doing this, but a more exciting prospect suggested itself: an expedition to Egypt. This was to be a joint venture, under the direction of Champollion and his Tuscan counterpart, Ippolito Rosellini. The boy in Robert Louis Stevenson's poem had turned into the man with the camel caravan, and nothing could stop him from seeing the pictures on the old walls.

Champollion first set eyes on Egypt, the 'bleached

coast of Africa' as he described it, on 18 August 1828. His Egyptological writings are familiar to scholars of the subject, but his other work is hardly known outside France. In the manner of the time but far in excess of it, he kept journals, recording his impressions of the country whose history he was in the process of recreating. He wrote endless letters home, and to his brother, and these are full of the seemingly inexhaustible energy of the man.

What he saw was a country still largely untouched by the influence of the West. The main exception was the rapid growth of the trade in antiquities to Europe, many of the exponents of which were suspicious of someone who was clearly out to pollute the pure waters of profit with the murky stream of scholarship. He reserves his choicest invective for these pests of dealers. He knows that monuments need to be copied and published before the agents of these vandals hack them to pieces to make a quick sale. 'In this way,' he says, 'they will be rescued from certain destruction at the threatening hands of ever more active savages.' By way of contrast, he calmly records the names of gods and kings, and it takes an effort to remember that Champollion was the first person since Horapollo who was in a position to do this. On almost every page of his diaries, he recorded his amazement at what he saw.

At the temple of Luxor, Champollion was able to study the pair of obelisks which stood before the first pylon, or monumental gateway. He expressed the hope that one of them would find its way to France. In 1836, four years after his death, the obelisk was shipped to Paris, where it is now in the Place de la Concorde. The poet Théophile Gautier was unable to resist penning some verses about the pair, now that

12. The temple of Luxor, with the twin of the obelisk transported to Paris.

they had been separated after more than 3,000 years together. He portrayed the Paris obelisk as weeping tears of granite, longing for its brother monument and the starry peace of the Egyptian night. The Luxor obelisk, he feels sure, is weeping identical tears, because it is not in Paris.

The Franco-Italian expedition lasted for fifteen months and went to the second cataract, which forms the southern frontier of Egypt. This was every bit as far as Napoleon's savants had achieved. On the return, there was an extended stay in the Valley of the Kings, where inscription after inscription awaited their decipherer. More than once, his companions found him unconscious or semi-conscious on the floor of one of the tombs. On 11 September 1829 Champollion wrote to his brother from Middle Egypt, 'My voyage of research is over and I am returning as quickly as possible towards Alexandria ... to find there both solace for my heart and repose for my body, for the latter of which I have no great need.' Solace for his heart he had earned, but he could not have been more wrong about the need to find repose for his body.

As a result of his journey, which had completely vindicated his decipherment, Champollion was elected in 1831 to the first chair of Egyptology in the world, at the Collège de France. This was an undoubted honour, but it came with daunting responsibilities: planning courses, recruiting assistants, a ceaseless programme of publication and an unremitting series of social events and official frustrations. Some of the old animosity towards him flared up again, in a way that had not happened when he was only one of a number of curators in the Louvre. Champollion could never be relaxed with his contemporaries and rivals. Even after his death one of his pupils, an Italian named Salvolini, was to steal several of his manuscripts and publish their discoveries as if they had been his own.

Scepticism about Champollion's work persisted for quite some time. In the middle of the 1820s Jean-François received a pompous letter from one Gustavus Seyffarth, explaining that the Frenchman was wrong about the hieroglyphs in every detail, and that he, Seyffarth, had hit upon the truth that he had missed. According to him, the key to the hieroglyphs was to be found in an alphabet created by Noah, which consisted of eighteen consonants and seven vowels corresponding to selected signs of the zodiac. This was going not from the known to the unknown, but from the unknown to the unknowable. Champollion's reply was a model of restraint, and he went back to his work. Seyffarth ended up in the United States, where he published a series of books devoted to his findings. These books were written in Latin, and in the publicity for his lectures he was happy to bill himself as the decipherer of Egyptian. In Champollion's circle, Seyffarth came to be known as the pseudo-Egyptian. There is an entry on him in that mine of antiquarian gossip *Who Was Who in Egyptology*. Otherwise the poor man is forgotten.

All Champollion's portraits show that he was chubby, but this is to put it in the flattering way that portraits are intended to do. His small daughter, whom he landed with the exotic name Zoraïde, he described as '*ma petite commère grasse à lard*' ('my little roly-poly chatterbox'). But the drawings and cartoons that come out of the Franco-Tuscan expedition reveal someone who was growing dangerously obese. The combination of a driven personality and an overweight body can be a fatal one, and there is little doubt that the

13. The birthplace of Champollion as it is now, with the large replica of the
Rosetta Stone set into the paving of the courtyard.

gruelling tour of Egypt exacted its price. At the end of 1831 the heart attacks began.

Two and a half years after his return from Egypt Champollion was dead. On 4 March 1832 he succumbed to a stroke or another heart attack, at the age of forty-one. Zoraïde was just eight. If her father had lasted as long as his elder brother, he would have lived to 1879. He is buried under a plain obelisk in the cemetery of Père Lachaise, Paris, close to some of the savants of Napoleon's mission. In the following years, towns and cities all over France would be queuing up to acquire their own rue or lycée Champollion. (Given Champollion's school record, the latter is ironic in the extreme.) There is a statue to the decipherer in the forecourt of the Collège de France, where for less than a year he held his chair. This professorship still exists. The centenary of the Dacier letter was marked in 1922 by a volume with forty-five contributors, and one can only imagine what the anniversary in 2022 will entail. The family house at Figeac is now a museum and a secular shrine; set into the floor of the courtyard is a large reproduction of the Rosetta Stone by the sculptor Joseph Kossuth. Egyptology, Champollion's other child, has claimed its father back.

5

'TO MAKE THEM LIVE AGAIN'

*I have turned over in my hand the titles of years whose history
was totally forgotten; the names of gods who have not had altars
these fifteen centuries, and I have gathered the tiniest pieces of
papyrus, scarcely drawing breath for fear of reducing them to
powder, the last and only memory of a king who during his
life maybe found himself all pent up in the immense palace of
Karnak.*

Jean-François Champollion, letter to his elder brother, 6 November 1824

How did the restless Frenchman come to be in the position
to recreate the history of his fragments of papyrus, or any
others for that matter? He had started from the same point as
Thomas Young, comparing the Greek names which appeared
on the stone with the Ptolemy and Cleopatra which had later
turned up on the Bankes obelisk. From this he was able to
build up the greater part of a hieroglyphic alphabet, which
he was able to enlarge by turning to copies of other inscriptions from Egypt which were beginning to reach Europe in
ever greater numbers. In particular, drawings and casts, or
squeeze impressions, from the great temple at Karnak, part
of ancient Thebes, produced the names of more Ptolemies
and several Roman emperors. Champollion was able to do

much the same for the commoner signs which appeared in the demotic register. These too tended to occur in sequences, spelling out the various Greek names which corresponded to the ones which appeared in the Greek register. It was this hieroglyphic and demotic alphabet which he announced with such confidence in the *Lettre à Monsieur Dacier*.

The real reason for Champollion's confidence did not feature in the Dacier letter. Twenty or so letters of an alphabet were a start, useful for spelling Greek names and things of that sort, but what about the other signs of the hieroglyphic script, the number of which ran into the hundreds or thousands? Obviously these could not be part of any alphabet. However, the young Frenchman now had the key to the way the rest of the script was put together. A week before the famous meeting at the academy, the temple of Karnak had given up a greater secret. On the walls and columns of the great hypostyle, the largest columned hall ever constructed, were cartouches containing a combination of four signs which kept repeating themselves. These took the form ○⚶⫯⫯. The likelihood was that these were the name of a king, almost certainly one from the many centuries before the Greeks began to rule the country. But which one was this, and where should decipherment start?

To understand the difficulties which faced Champollion at this point it will help if we try to get to grips with the ways in which writing works, and how it came into being. We have already seen that the development of early scripts was an interest of Warburton in England, and then of Zoëga in Denmark and Italy. Champollion was familiar with these men's ideas, but he needed to go further. In essence there have only ever been three ideas in the story of writing: the picture, the pun and the cartoon. It is a commonplace that writing began with pictures of the natural world, but being commonplace does not make an idea untrue. A picture of a bird or a fish or a crescent moon can readily bring to mind the word itself, no matter what the underlying language. More elaborately, a picture of a man firing an arrow at a panda conveys a message, although it is a message which is not defined in time or place. It could mean, 'I shot a panda', 'with luck I may shoot a panda', 'shoot pandas before they eat leaves', or a range of other concepts, provided that they are something to do with pandas and shooting. There is meaning of a sort here, because the elements in the picture correspond to elements in the physical world, but the circumstances and the details have to be left vague. Once the person who made the picture has moved on, his exact meaning can only be guessed.

What about words which cannot be expressed in pictures? Concepts such as 'belief' or 'reliability' are extremely difficult to convey pictorially, except by means of the complicated symbolic allegories which Victorian painters were fond of creating. In practice, this is not a solution. This is where the pun comes in. Belief cannot be drawn, but a picture of a bee next to a leaf can be. In this step, the literal meanings of the pictures are made to take second place to their sound-values, and as a result such puns can only be valid for the language for which they are designed: bees and leaves will not do the same job in French or German, for example. Nevertheless, this phonetic leap happens in hieroglyphs, and also in the Near Eastern cuneiform of southern Iraq, which is probably the earliest script known. It is also found in Chinese. In these cases, in the Old World, there is always the possibility that the idea of phonetic puns travelled from one centre of civilisation to another, and therefore that it was invented only once. However, the same technique is also found in the script of the Maya from Mexico. Since as far as we know the Maya were not in contact with the Old World, they must have invented the method independently. The likelihood is that pun-writing is universal to the human mind, and it can be seen in all societies where writing has developed. I was recently at a birthday party for a colleague named Postgate, and the cake turned out to be decorated with a post on top of a gate. The idea also appears in heraldry, where, for instance, the name Burton can be conveyed by a thistle (*burr*) on top of a barrel (*tun*). Here the pictures also fulfil an emblematic purpose: if your name is Burton, this is the shield for you.

In a similar way, the notion of 'queenship' is impossible to convey as a picture, because it is essentially abstract. But a drawing of a woman with a crown on her head next to one of a ship would do the job, if only in English. The first picture in this group can be called an ideogram, since it conveys the notion of a woman ruler and only invites you to supply the word for it, but the ship in this instance is there purely for its phonetic value. This sort of combination is close to what Champollion was about to find in the cartouche from Karnak, and it is typical of hieroglyphic writing.

The logical extension of the pun principle is to forget about the pictorial aspect of things altogether. This can be seen to an extent in the hieroglyphic alphabet which Champollion drew up, where, for example, an outstretched hand is simply the sign for *d*, and all resemblance to a hand is entirely accidental. (The Egyptian word for hand originally contained this sound, but that word was soon replaced by a completely different one, and the connection between the sign and the sound had long been lost.) The hieroglyphs remained pictorial, but the demotic script did not, since there the signs are reduced to abstract shapes. Our own alphabet, with its twenty-six letters, has lost all memory of its pictorial origins. Yet the alphabet which we use also began as a series of pictures, probably taken from Egyptian hieroglyphs. However, rather than keeping the sounds which they had in the Egyptian system, the adapters applied the values which were familiar from their own language, a Semitic tongue related to Hebrew or a similar dialect spoken somewhere in Syria or Palestine. Here it was the opening sounds of the pictures which were chosen, rather than the whole words, using a principle which is known as acrophony. In this way, a picture of an ox's head (Semitic *aleph*, meaning 'ox') was used to convey the sound *a*, while waves of water (Semitic *mayim*, meaning 'water') became *m*. Today, a capital *A*, turned upside down, still looks a little like the ox's head from which it came, and the letter *m* does bear some resemblance to watery waves. But most of the time we are unaware of this, and the picture element means nothing: to us, the sound-values of our twenty-six letters are nothing more than a convention.

The third idea in the development of writing is the cartoon. This occurs when pictorial signs are combined to make a more complex idea, and this is normally done without reference to any sound-values. Truth, or reliability, is another concept that is impossible to convey purely pictorially, but Chinese gets round this problem by writing the character for 'man' next to the character for 'speech' (this is pictured as words coming out of a stylised mouth). Reliability is a man standing by his word, and here we have a drawing to this effect. This has nothing to do with the sounds of the individual signs (in this example, the Chinese for 'reliability' is not the same as the Chinese words for 'man-speech'). It is the combination of characters, and their arrangement, which convey the meaning. In theory, cartoons of this sort are international, since they are independent of spoken language. They are used nowadays on packets or containers, where they are supposed to convey worldwide sentiments such as 'dry clean only', 'no dogs', 'breakable glass' or 'this packet of peanuts may contain nuts'. In practice, these symbols are often completely obscure, and we end up wishing the manufacturers would go back to putting the message in words. It may be for this reason that the cartoon is used less in early writing systems than the pun. It does appear from time to time in hieroglyphs, however, and here too it was Champollion who was the first to make sense of what was happening.

We left Jean-François Champollion peering at his copy of the cartouche from the temple of Karnak, which we recall looked like this: ⊙𝍖𝍏𝍏. The last two signs in this group were identical (𝍏), and Champollion already knew from his alphabet that they had to be the letter *s*. The same letter regularly appeared as the final sign in the name of King Ptolemy, whose name in Greek was pronounced Ptolemaios. The first sign, ⊙, had also turned up in Champollion's counts of the individual signs, and he had a good suspicion that it signified the disc of the sun. However, he had not been able to give it a sound-value in his alphabet, and it was becoming more and more likely that this sign was not a straightforward phonetic one. The middle sign, 𝍖, was more enigmatic, but it did recur several times on the hieroglyphic text of the stone. In each case, judging from the positions in the lines which it occupied, it seemed to correspond to words in the Greek section of the text such as 'birthday', 'being born' or something of that sort. In reality this sign represents three fox skins tied together as an amulet to protect women in childbirth. An interesting detail, no doubt, but how were these signs supposed to be pronounced?

The answer lay in Coptic, as the medieval Arabic writers had known. Athanasius Kircher, the polymath Jesuit, was the first in modern times to suggest that this language had also been the language of the Pharaohs, and others, particularly Georg Zoëga and Thomas Young, had followed this line. Champollion had learned the basics of this language from an Egyptian priest in Paris. As part of his interest in anything which could shed light on the stone, he was increasingly studying the Greek papyri from Egypt, most of which were legal contracts containing everyday Egyptian names written in a script which held no secrets, since knowledge of Greek had never been lost. Many of these names could be shown to make sense in Coptic, or more accurately a slightly earlier form of it. In Coptic the word for 'sun' was *rê* or *ra*, and the word for 'to bear' a child was *mise* or *mes*. The Frenchman had read everything about ancient Egypt that he could lay his hands on, and one of his sources was all that was left of a history of the country written at the start of the second century BC by a native priest named Manetho. Manetho wrote in Greek for the new rulers of his country, but his original text is lost. The summaries of the summaries of his book, which are all that have come down to us, give lists of most of the Pharaohs, although more than a few of these names had become corrupted over the centuries. Among Manetho's listing for what he termed the Nineteenth and Twentieth Dynasties were several kings called Ramesses, and *ra-mes-ses*, Champollion realised, was the exact reading of the group from Karnak. It was true that there was no sign corresponding to the vowel between the last two *s*'s, but Champollion was familiar with scripts like Hebrew and Arabic, where vowels could be regularly ignored, especially when they were short and unemphasised. Ramesses, then, was the king who had left his name all over the great hall of columns at Karnak.

Champollion then turned to his copy of a similar group, also a king's name. This was written 𓅝 𓏶𓏤. The second group was more or less identical to the one in the middle of the first name, and this, he now knew, had the value *mes* or something very like it. The sign at the beginning was a sacred ibis, and Champollion was aware from his boyhood that the Egyptians had revered a god of writing and wisdom, whose emblem was an ibis. This was Thoth, or Thot as he could also appear in Greek sources. Again, Manetho was there to tell him that there had been a series of kings in the dynasty before Ramesses who had borne the name Tuthmosis. The final –*s* which appears in this spelling of the name is simply a feature of Greek. In Coptic, *Thotmose* would mean '[The pagan god] Thoth is born.' If this was a coincidence, it was a coincidence too many. Champollion knew that this had to be the way ahead. At the time of the *Lettre à Monsieur Dacier*, these readings were still inspired guesses rather than a proof, and this was one reason why he was reluctant to use them at that stage. But a greater reason for his reticence was that to publish this discovery too early would be to give his rivals the clue they were looking for. There would be nothing to prevent them saying that they had thought of it for themselves, and some of them were quite capable of adding that Champollion had stolen the idea from them in the first place.

Vital things followed from these two names, Ramesses and Tuthmosis. First, it was clear that the Coptic language would be the key to reading many of the individual words. The old idea that this language was descended from the speech of the Pharaohs was true after all. It was this which gave the essential phonetic values which on the whole had eluded Young. The Englishman had succeeded in identifying the meanings of quite a few words, but he had been unable to give sound-values to most of his groups. Second, it was clear that the use of phonetic signs was not confined to the Graeco-Roman period, as Young and others still imagined, since it was now present in far earlier cartouches. Finally, and most important of all, these breakthroughs showed Champollion the true nature of the hieroglyphic system. It was not alphabetic throughout, nor was it entirely phonetic, although groups such as *mes* seemed to be intended for the purpose of writing syllables as opposed to individual sounds. The use of the sign for 'sun', however, was closer to what was described above as an ideogram, a sign which conveys a concept rather than something which is used purely for its sound-value. As we have seen, Champollion had studied Chinese during his teenage years, unlike his rivals. He knew that the Chinese script was a complex one which combined ideograms and phonetic elements in varying ways, although it contained no alphabet as such. Chinese writing went way back into antiquity, and there was a fair chance that early Egyptian had developed along similar lines. This was the way that Champollion's researches now led him, and this time the god of writing was not going to let him down.

Champollion also came to terms with another kind of sign which was more puzzling. Nowadays these are known as determinatives, and beginners in Egyptology are required to learn a list of thirty or forty of them, as soon as they have mastered the characters of the hieroglyphic alphabet. Determinatives go at the ends of most words, but are not pronounced. Instead, they indicate the category or type of the word they qualify. There are determinatives for wooden objects, buildings, ships, animals, foreign countries, gods, things that are nasty, and so on. They are essential, in that strictly speaking the Egyptians did not write the vowels of their language, but only the consonants. As a result there are words which are completely different in meaning that would look identical if it were not for the determinative at the end. In Egyptian, the words for 'tax', 'horse' and 'twin' look alike phonetically, since they share the same consonants. (The reason for this is that all three words come from a root which means 'yoke'. Twins come in pairs, like yoked animals; horses in Egypt were originally paired to draw chariots; and a tax is an imposition, like a yoke laid upon somebody's shoulders.) A writing system which could not distinguish between words like these would lead to serious misunderstandings within a very short time. Determinatives provide a neat answer to this problem: the twin gets a person sign, the horse an animal's skin and the tax a picture of a roll of papyrus, to show that it is something recorded.

Determinatives also carry the message 'the word you are looking at is now finished'. This too is important, since hiero-glyphic and demotic, like most ancient scripts, did not leave gaps between individual words. To early investigators of the Rosetta Stone, determinatives will have been the equivalent of junk DNA: something which is clearly there, but which does not appear to have a function, since there were no words in the Greek text of the stone that these signs could correspond to. Determinatives are not a regular feature of Chinese, or any other script that Champollion could have known, and his solution to the problem of these signs is probably his greatest single achievement.

From this point Champollion was able to stop puzzling over the hieroglyphs and start reading them. The Egypt of the Pharaohs was being reborn. As the ancient Egyptians themselves put it, 'To speak the name of the dead is to make them live again', and this is what Champollion did for them. But in reality he did more than this. In his work on the stone he not only deciphered ancient Egyptian. He deciphered the story of writing as well.

HOW TO GO ABOUT DECIPHERING

- Start by counting the number of signs.

    If this comes to 20 or 30, the script is almost certainly an alphabet.

    If the total is more like 80 or 100, the script is probably syllabic (see pp. 102–3).

    If the total comes to several hundreds, the script will be a mixture of ideograms and phonetic signs arranged in various ways (see pp. 81–90).

    This is true of Egyptian hieroglyphs, and almost all other early writing systems.

- Look for word divisions, or other ways of distinguishing individual words (see pp. 88–9 and 101–2).

- Look for combinations of signs which repeat themselves and which may correspond to names of people, gods, rivers or places.

- Numbering systems are often easy to identify, but in general they are less helpful, because they tend to be abstract, telling us little or nothing about the underlying language. None the less, they can be useful landmarks when analysing a text.

If there is a bilingual text
- Starting with the known language of the bilingual, list proper names and significant phrases which repeat themselves or are important in other ways.
- Try matching these significant items with combinations of signs in the unknown language. Not all bilinguals reproduce themselves exactly, since there may be different emphases in the different languages. But overall proper names and similar words are some of the most likely ones to be repeated, since they are vital to what the text is setting out to record.
- Signs which appear frequently, and in words of differing lengths or types, may be phonetic. This is particularly true when a language needs to spell names which are not from that language. Greek names spelt out in hieroglyphs, and in the demotic register of the Rosetta Stone, represented the first breakthroughs in finding out the phonetic structure of Egyptian (see Chapters 3, 4 and 5 above).
- When several phonetic signs are known, try to identify grammatical elements, such as plurals, feminine endings and personal pronouns. Do these match any known language? In the case of the Rosetta Stone, resemblances with Coptic soon started to make themselves felt, and this was a very significant advance.

If there is no bilingual text

- Ask to be reborn as Michael Ventris (see pp.101–6). If this request is refused, there is no alternative but to tackle the script from within, spotting things such as corrections by scribes and counting frequencies of individual signs. If a sign is common at the beginning of words, for example, it may turn out to be a vowel. If it is common at the end, it may be some kind of grammatical ending, such as a mark of gender or a plural. If there are no changes of this sort, the language may be one like Chinese, where individual words hardly ever vary.

- Try to reconstruct a grid, or some similar pattern, in which the individual signs are grouped by families, perhaps sharing the same consonant but with different vowels, or showing what may be the plural or feminine versions of other signs (see pp. 102–4).

- Build up a list of repeated combinations of signs which may be names of people, gods or places. If a particular group is common in texts from one place but not from others, could it be the name of that place? Have place names survived into modern times, or are they preserved in ancient sources in other languages which we can read? The UK, for example, has place and river names which survive from Celtic, and the Americas have names in Algonquin, Maya and many other Amerindian languages.

- Try matching known place or personal names with combinations suspected to be these names. If the matches are correct, some of the phonetic values of the signs should become clear.

More general points
- If a decipherment is going nowhere, this is probably because it is wrong. Most would-be decipherments end up this way. If, on the other hand, things start to snowball, with more and more possibilities turning into probabilities, this is a good sign that you are on the right lines.
- Some decipherments are simply not possible. This is especially true when the number of texts is down to one or two, or the surviving examples are too short. In cases like this, somebody could make a correct decipherment, but we would never know this, because there is no new material on which to test the result. Much effort has been wasted on one-offs such as the notorious Phaestos Disk from Crete. At the moment, there is no parallel for this text, and so no way of checking the various attempts to crack this inscription.
- The most important script still undeciphered is that of the Indus Valley civilisation, dating from the third millennium BC, in what is now Pakistan. The number of signs in this script suggests that it too is a mixture of ideographic and phonetic elements. So far there is no bilingual and the texts are noticeably short. The underlying language is unknown, although some have suggested that it is part of the Dravidian family, which is nowadays found in southern India in languages such as Tamil. A longer text, or a bilingual, would make a decipherment much easier.
- Finally, it can be possible to read an ancient language but not understand it. So far, this is true of the Etruscan language, which is written in a form of the Greek alphabet, and the language of Meroe in the Sudan, which is written in two alphabets derived from Egyptian (see p. 118). Here,

14. A mystery still unsolved: one of the undeciphered seal-impressions from the city of Harappa in the Indus Valley.

in order to make real progress, it is vital to find which other languages, ancient or modern, the mystery language is related to. Otherwise, progress is halting and too imprecise to carry the day. In the case of Etruscan there are bilingual texts, but these have not helped as much as was first hoped.

....

6

THE RETURN OF THE LIGHT

On this scroll there are two spells. If you read the first spell you will orbit the heavens, the earth and the underworld, the mountains and the seas. You will discover what the birds of the sky and the crawling creatures speak, all of them. You will behold the fishes of the deep, even though there are twenty-one divine cubits of water over them. If you read the second spell, even if you are in the underworld, you will resume your form on earth. You will see the sun rising in the heaven together with his retinue of gods, and the moon at its invisible birth.

from the demotic story of Setne (first century BC)

Champollion was a Frenchman, and the French have always taken to Egyptology. Napoleon retreated from Egypt, and the country eventually found itself part of the British Empire, although for most of the period of British rule it was governed in a semi-detached sort of way. Intellectually and culturally, however, Egypt fell into the French sphere, and anyone who takes a tour of the slowly disappearing nineteenth-century buildings in Cairo – perhaps making a convenient start in the rue Champollion – will recognise that the city looked to Paris and Rome rather than London. The law of modern Egypt is a modified form of the Code Napoléon, not British case law or the Islamic *shari'a*.

This is as it should be. Modern Egyptians feel an affinity with Mediterranean culture as well as with their Arab neighbours, and the influence of French literature on modern Egyptian writers is great. The indirect legacy of Napoleon's invasion is still there in the country, and it may well be that the resemblances to France go further back. For most of its history, ancient Egypt was a self-contained land, with relatively secure frontiers. Seas and deserts protected it, but there was a weak point at its north-east corner, where the coastal roads from Palestine came in. This was where almost all its invaders entered the country, in spite of the Pharaohs' attempts to fortify the area with canals, moats and defensive walls. It was a highly centralised state, with a natural capital at Memphis, where the streams of the Delta joined the valley of the Nile. It was run by a sun king who deliberately used his splendour to focus the loyalties of his subjects on to his person. The influence and wealth of the royal court made the country the cultural leader of much of the Near East, and what went on there was envied and copied by poorer and more provincial neighbours. The self-confidence of its culture attracted skilled immigrants from all over the Near East, and later the Greek world. Many ancient Egyptians must have been born into families who had journeyed there to share in that culture. Once there, they adopted the language and the religion of their hosts. The whole place was full of the hieroglyphic equivalent of what the French term *la gloire*, at least until a determined enemy appeared, in which case resistance tended to evaporate. But Egypt it was in spite of this, and Egypt it remained.

Although Thomas Young did not know it, the Rosetta Stone had made up its mind to be deciphered by a Frenchman. The result was the first major breakthrough in our knowledge of the ancient world. Champollion's decipherment was not, strictly speaking, the first of its kind. His own teacher, Silvestre de Sacy, had solved the mysteries of the Sassanid script from Persia, and it could be that it was the determination to be the only decipherer in town that turned him against his Egypt-obsessed pupil. In 1754 another Frenchman, Abbé Barthélemy, had cracked the alphabetic inscriptions from the city of Palmyra in the Syrian desert, racing ahead of an English rival in the process. These were considerable achievements, but the Palmyrene inscriptions were written in a variant of the Aramaic script, which was relatively well known. Palmyrene, too, turned out to be a branch of the Semitic family, which includes Hebrew and Arabic, and this made progress fairly straightforward. Nor did the Sassanid and Palmyra texts have anything like the glamour of the Rosetta Stone. Hieroglyphs were far more complex and much more alluring. Scholars for fifteen centuries had devoted the better part of their lives to their mysteries. What Champollion did was to produce the first 'spectacular' in the history of code-breaking.

Before Champollion, the ancient voices from the ancient world that could be heard were from Greece, Rome and the Bible. Now the Egyptians were beginning to speak with their own voice. This was a triumph for understanding, but it was clear even in Champollion's own lifetime that parts of the new story would turn out to be divisive. Before the decipherment, Champollion's work on the chronology of ancient Egypt had started to provoke the Catholic Church, which had an uneasy relationship with the revolution in France and those who supported it. As his work progressed and he found more and more Pharaohs with higher and higher regnal years, it became increasingly clear to Champollion that the traditional timescale taught by the Church was too short. The thirty dynasties given by the chronicler Manetho could not be reconciled with the received dates for Old Testament figures such as Abraham and Solomon. The Church retaliated by declaring that the advanced dates for Egyptian civilisation which this pipsqueak was proposing were far too close to the period of Noah's flood, which as everyone knew was a time of primitive ignorance. In the case of the Dendera zodiac, however, which Champollion had shown to be very late by Egyptian standards, the paradoxical result was that the same pipsqueak was hailed by the Church as a champion of its cause. Here we have a foretaste of the bitter debate about science and religion which was to occupy much of the nineteenth century, the echoes of which are still with us in the twenty-first. Champollion found something of the controversy and opposition which were later to beset Darwin in the realm of evolution. The authority of Holy Writ was a mighty opponent to take on. In his letters to Angelica Palli, his Zelmire, the iconoclast in Champollion keeps returning to this theme:

Philosophers, or people who call themselves that, have cried out against me, saying that my hieroglyphic system is pure invention in order to suck up to the clergy and curry favour with the powers. So here we have the same philosophers turned my detractors, without bothering to examine whether my discoveries are founded on incontestable facts or not. On the other hand ... I have found, by applying my same hieroglyphic alphabet, that there really were temples and palaces in Egypt, masterpieces of architecture, which were built 2,300 years before Christ, in other words 4,127 years ago ... As a result I find both sides ranged against me.

As decipherments go, Champollion's is the most glamorous. The hieroglyphs had been a subject of fascination for centuries, in the way that most other scripts had not. Champollion was also a child of the romantic era, and this shows in his prose as well as in his tumultuous life. He is the Byron of scholarship, and he is also an outsider like Keats. His intellectual talent, combined with the years of detailed research which led to his breakthrough, holds us in awe, and his early death moves us. Other decipherments, such as that of the various languages written in the cuneiform script, have many of the ingredients of an adventure story. But the solving of the Rosetta Stone outclasses all of these with its resonance and romance.

Could Egyptian have been deciphered without the Rosetta Stone? The answer is probably yes, but slowly and far less spectacularly. Champollion could have picked up enough clues in his work on other texts to start him on the right road, and a breakthrough might have happened in his lifetime, given his energy and commitment. Alternatively, we would have had to wait for a later name, in which case the Frenchman would now be known as the godfather of Egyptology rather than its father. But it is hard not to toy with the idea that Champollion and the stone were made for each other by some muse who concerns herself with things such as these. Like the hieroglyphic script which forms its subject, we are dealing with the most pictorial of decipherments.

It is true that Champollion had hardly any precedents to go on, and most of the time he was forced to work in an atmosphere of rivalry and distrust. But the big advantage was that the Rosetta Stone was a bilingual text, or more accurately a trilingual. There are probably two things which help a decipherer most. One is to find clear divisions between the words of an inscription, because then it is possible to start analysing the words, knowing where they begin and end and how they behave. Champollion did not have word divisions, though his unravelling of the determinatives later gave him the same information. But he did have his bilingual, and this is the greatest thing a decipherer can be given. The officers of General Menou recognised this immediately, when they looked at the Greek text on the stone and sent it to the savants in Cairo.

Another advantage was that Champollion had a fairly good idea what the Egyptian language would turn out to be. His knowledge of Coptic and his familiarity with Egyptian names recorded in Greek gave him the clues he needed. This too was a starting point. These advantages, together with the enormous mental powers which he possessed, were what enabled him to unlock the secrets of the stone.

If we think of decipherment purely as an intellectual exercise, the peak of achievement probably belongs not to Champollion, but to an architect named Michael Ventris (1922–56). Ventris was the man who found the key to the Linear B tablets which had been excavated in Crete and parts of the Greek mainland. Some of these tablets had been studied for half a century without any progress being made, and one expert concluded that they were simply undecipherable. This soon became the standard view. There were divisions between the words, however, and this gave cause for a little optimism, but the language of the tablets was unknown, and so was their script. Most of the texts were short, which only added to the difficulty. Ventris tackled this daunting task by a method which was completely new. Like Nelson at the Nile, he had no charts. He suspected from the number of signs that the writing was a syllabary, perhaps with combinations ending in a vowel, such as *ta, to, tu*, etc. He then patiently went through all the tablets, noting where the ancient scribes had corrected themselves. Perhaps there were cases where *ta*, for example, had been altered to *tu*. This way it might be possible to reconstruct families of signs. Bit by bit, Ventris was able to build up a grid, with unknown vowels at the top and equally unknown consonants at the side. But how could he decide which consonants and vowels were which?

Ventris now turned to exactly the same technique that Champollion had used: try to identify proper names. Proper names, such as Ptolemy and Ramesses, are often the only traces of an ancient culture that survive, and this is particularly true of place names. Many of the tablets Ventris studied came from the site of Knossos in Crete, and in those texts there was a commonly occurring group of three signs. As it happened, these three signs all stood in one of the vowel columns which Ventris had drawn up in his notebooks, and he suggested for the group the reading *ko-no-so*, or Knossos. This fixed one of the vowels, *o*, and three consonants, *k*, *n* and *s*. Other groups now started to suggest themselves, and Ventris's grid slowly began to make sounds as well as pictures. The sounds which came out were the one language that everybody, including Ventris, had agreed was out of the question. Linear B was Greek.

15. Angelic: Michael Ventris, decipherer of Linear B, *c.* 1945.

Dramatic proof of the decipherment of the Cretan script came with the discovery of a new tablet, showing pictures of tripods with varying numbers of handles and captions next to them. These captions made perfect sense in an early form of Greek: tripods with two, four or no ears. Ventris himself was to call the tripod tablet 'a sort of Rosetta Stone', but it was a Rosetta Stone which came after the event, not before it. The history of decipherment, however, is a fraught one, as we have seen with Young and Champollion. There were mutterings that Ventris must have known about the thing all along, by critics who had run out of anything better to say. Scepticism about Ventris's decipherment persisted well into the 1970s, in spite of the clear evidence that he could never have set eyes on the tripod tablet when he drew up his grid. This sort of thing appeals to the kind of academic who makes a career out of bending over backwards to deny the obvious. Now the scepticism is finished and Ventris's achievement is recognised for what it is.

The techniques used on Linear B are close to some of those used by professional cryptographers, and this is one reason why this decipherment is so admired. Like Champollion, Ventris died young, in his case as a result of a car accident in 1956. This increases the poignancy of his work. But the truth is that the tablets themselves are limited in what they can tell us, being for the most part inventories. So far we have no literature in Linear B, no personal letters and no history. These may have been written on other materials which have perished. In the case of Egypt, we have precisely this sort of material, in the form of papyrus, and with it we can gain access to the humanity of the ancient Egyptians. It is Champollion's devotion to the texts on the Rosetta Stone that brought this

16. Diabolical: Yuri Knorosov, decipherer of Maya hieroglyphs, with a companion, *c.* 1960.

humanity back to us, and this will be the subject of the next chapter. Decipherment is not a purely intellectual exercise; it is the restoration of people's thoughts and lives.

The most important decipherment of recent years is the work of a Russian scholar, Yuri Valentinovich Knorosov (or Knorozov; 1922–99). Knorosov laboured under the Soviet system, but this at least allowed him to work on marginal subjects which were not politically challenging, and he found himself drawn to the writing system of the Maya Indians from Yucatán and neighbouring parts of Central America. He lacked most of the facilities which his colleagues in the West took for granted, and he had no choice but to work in isolation. Marxist ideology was imposed on his work by his superiors. At first, his work was ignored outside his native land. The fact that he wrote in Russian may not have helped in this respect, especially at the height of the Cold War, but there was a deeper reason for the neglect. In the case of this script the conceptual framework, as we have termed it, was not in place. With the Maya, as with Egyptian hieroglyphs, progress was held up by what we can only describe as a mystically correct orthodoxy: the idea that the script was not a normal means of sharing information, but was really a series of meditations about the meaning of the universe. The Maya, after all, were supposed to be the philosophers of ancient Mexico, unlike the rest of their bloodthirsty neighbours. Their celestial musings could never be understood by anyone who was not steeped in the mysticism of the past, a past which had vanished beyond recall. It was precisely this sort of thing which held back progress on Egyptian hieroglyphics throughout the centuries before the Rosetta Stone was discovered. This was where Athanasius Kircher had been marooned, and others before him. Maya studies were trapped in much the same dead end that Egyptology had found itself in until the days of Zoëga and Young. The analogy with Egyptian hieroglyphics is striking.

With the Maya script there was also the problem of a dialogue of the deaf, similar to the one that Horapollo may have had with his informants. A sixteenth-century Spanish bishop of Yucatán, Diego de Landa, made use of a native speaker of Maya who was literate, and asked him something which came naturally to a European: could he go through the Maya alphabet? The Maya script had no alphabet, but it did have signs for syllables. When the Maya heard the Spaniard coming out with the sounds *ah*, *be*, *se*, etc., he naturally assumed that he was being asked about these syllables, and he wrote down the corresponding signs. He was telling the truth as he knew it, but the resulting 'Maya alphabet' became a false friend which only served to stifle greater understanding. Landa's notes were discredited and fell into neglect. This did away with the one pointer to the solution that the Maya script had been a phonetic system after all. The idea took over that the glyphs could only be aids to speculation, a sort of cosmological doodling.

It was not until the middle of the twentieth century that Yuri Knorosov succeeded in sweeping away this misunderstanding and showed the true nature of this writing, rehabilitating Landa's Mayan informant in the process. Knorosov was an outsider who was not part of the esoteric orthodoxy and its mindset. From this start, he was able to identify several place names and other words which gave him the true values of more phonetic signs. Another breakthrough was to pin down the modern Maya dialect which was the closest to the language of the inscriptions, since the ancient language is still spoken in that part of Central America. Maya history now started to be reborn, with kings, dynasties and events which could be dated to precise days of the week, thanks to the accuracy of the Maya calendar. Diego de Landa's forgotten and misunderstood notes turned out to be for Knorosov what the Rosetta Stone had been for Champollion.

Using his insights, younger colleagues in America then turned to a group of signs which was commonly found on the rims of pottery mugs, and which was otherwise believed to be a thought about the meaning of space-time or something else along those lines. According to Knorosov's decipherment, the true reading of this group could only be *u cacao*, 'the person in question's cocoa'. This may seem banal, but cocoa-drinking had ritual significance among the Maya aristocracy, so the philosophical content of this discovery remained respectable enough. Cocoa could be mystically correct too.

The Soviets long refused permission for Knorosov to visit the lands he had studied in their libraries, and it was not until 1990 that he was allowed to travel to Central America. During his visit he received a phone call from a surprisingly well-read death squad, who were concerned that his work was raising the Maya's self-awareness and making them discontented with their lot, namely being exterminated. The Russian was given seventy-two hours to get on a plane. Never can the point that decipherment and national identity are intermingled have been made so graphically, or so chillingly. Knorosov was forced to return to St Petersburg, but he at least had the satisfaction of knowing that his life's work had been correct. He died of pneumonia in a hospital corridor at the age of seventy-six. The one published photograph of

Yuri Knorosov is intriguing: it makes him look almost devilish, and the impression is strengthened by the fact that he is holding a singularly malevolent cat. The contrast with the serene portraits of Michael Ventris could not be greater.

To tell the disappointing truth, the decipherment of the Yucatán script shows the Maya to have been little different from the rest of their neighbours. They too spent their lives making war, sacrificing captive chiefs and ritually letting blood out of their more painful body parts as an offering to the insatiable gods. Much of the detached philosophising of their older image has gone the way of the cocoa. But this is not a comment on Knorosov or his achievement. He too looked on the truth behind the mysteries, and this makes him part of the legacy of Champollion.

7

THE HEIRS OF JEAN-FRANÇOIS

The learned scribes of the age that came after the gods, those who foretold the future, their names have become everlasting ... Man decays, his body is dust, and all his kindred are no more. But a book makes him remembered ... The children of others are given to them, to be their heirs, as if they had been their own.

from Papyrus Chester Beatty IV, *In Praise of Learned Scribes* (c. 1200 BC)

Egyptian has the longest recorded history of any of the world's languages. Short hieroglyphic texts are now known from around 3200 BC, and the last, as we saw in the opening chapter, dates to AD 394. If we add the sources from the Coptic stage, when the hieroglyphs were replaced by the Greek alphabet but the language remained recognisably the same, we have a further 1,200 years of Egyptian to go. This makes forty-seven centuries, possibly more, before the language of the Pharaohs finally disappeared and gave way to Arabic. In the world of long-lived languages, Egyptian's nearest rivals are Greek (thirty-four centuries, but with a break of several centuries between Mycenaean times and the appearance of the alphabet) and Chinese (thirty-two centuries, with no break). One day these rivals may overtake Egypt's record, since they are still being spoken, but we will have to wait more than a thousand years to see this happen. It was this unique span of time which the stone brought back to us.

Linguists are also interested in Egyptian because it managed to change its spots halfway through its history. The earlier phases of the language, Old and Middle Egyptian, make use of inflections and changes of structure which rather remind us of a tightly controlled language such as Latin. This form of Egyptian continued to be written long after the colloquial language had moved on, and the hieroglyphic register on the stone was also composed in it. In the middle of the fourteenth century BC, however, this particular dam bursts, and the spoken form of the language starts to get into print. It is no accident that this change corresponds to the reign of the most iconoclastic of the Pharaohs, Akhenaten, who set out to change traditional Egyptian religion and much else besides. The new form of the language which appears at this point is termed Late Egyptian, and it stands to the Latin of the earlier phases much as modern Italian does. The verbal system is freer, and more attuned to subtle differences of tense and mood, and the tight word order of Middle Egyptian is abandoned in favour of something more immediate. Late Egyptian is the ancestor of demotic, the shorthand script found on the middle register of the Rosetta Stone. This in turn developed into Coptic, and it was the Coptic language which gave Champollion many of the answers he had been looking for.

As Homer put it, as is the race of leaves, so is the race of men. One generation flourishes, and another comes to an end, until another spring comes. Jean-François Champollion began the modern science of Egyptology, decoding the hieroglyphic script and making a promising start on demotic. But these could only be foundations, and it fell to others to build on them.

In addition to hieroglyphic and demotic, the scripts found on the stone, there is a cursive form of hieroglyphs known as hieratic, in which most letters and business documents were written until demotic arrived to take its place. Hieratic texts needed to be written quickly on material such as papyrus, and this accounts for the way that hieratic soon began to diverge from the hieroglyphs from which it originated: much of the pictorial nature of the script was sacrificed to speed. One of the pioneers in the deciphering of hieratic was English, a man name Charles Goodwin (1817–78). Goodwin earned his living as a lawyer and ended up as a judge in Shanghai, but in his spare time he transformed the study of hieratic. In demotic, however, the giant of the nineteenth century is undoubtedly the German Heinrich Brugsch (1827–94). At one point this tireless scholar was offered Champollion's chair at the Collège de France, but this stirred the German authorities into giving him one of his own at Göttingen. He founded one of the leading journals in the field, and then contributed 115 articles to it, while his list of published books, some of them stretching to six or seven volumes, is truly daunting. He also found time to produce a surprisingly readable autobiography.

Much of the nineteenth century was devoted to the rediscovery of Egypt's past. Egypt was now accessible to European expeditions, and these began to come to terms with the enormous scale of the remains waiting to be explored. Here the French had been the pioneers with the Italians, but the state of Prussia was also determined to make its impact on the growing subject. The years 1842–5 saw the great mission to Egypt and Nubia that was headed by Richard Lepsius. This expedition went far south into the Sudan, and was the first to realise the potential of this still relatively unexplored sub-continent. Lepsius, whose portrait shows him to have been something of a Wagnerian figure, turns out to be the author of no fewer than 142 works of Egyptology, which is the more remarkable since he was a slow beginner in the subject. He refused to learn Egyptian until Champollion's grammar had seen the light, but he was soon able to show that the Frenchman had got it right, and that other claims were baseless. He went on to oversee the building of the Berlin Museum, and was present at the state opening of the Suez Canal in 1869. He was eventually knighted by the Bavarians. Egyptology was joining the European elite. What is more, the sheer scale of the monuments and objects which were preserved in Egypt was now beginning to be grasped, and it was daunting.

The pioneer of archaeology in Egypt itself is another larger-than-life Frenchman, Auguste Mariette (1821–81). Mariette taught briefly at a school in England before going to Coventry to try his hand at ribbon manufacturing, but Egyptology soon claimed him. In 1850 he set foot in Egypt, ostensibly looking for manuscripts to buy. Instead, he started excavating the Serapeum, the burial place of several dynasties of deceased bulls known as the Apis. His discoveries at this site made his name, although he was not averse to speed-ing up the pace of excavation by resorting to gunpowder. He then went on to excavate at scores of other places. His greatest contribution to the subject is probably his creation of the first museum in Egypt itself, and the recognition of the importance of the country's archaeological heritage which this implied. The present-day Cairo Museum followed after

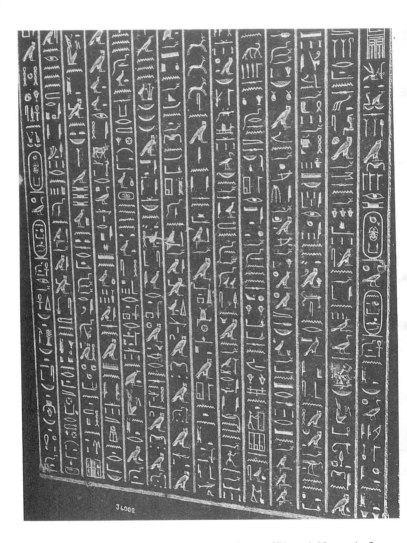

36002

17. Hieroglyphs at their finest: a customs-decree of Pharaoh Nectanebo I from the city of Naucratis in the Delta, 380 BC.

OFFICIAL HIERATIC OF THE TWENTIETH DYNASTY
WITH TRANSCRIPTION

LITERARY DEMOTIC OF THE THIRD CENTURY B.C.
WITH TRANSCRIPTION

18. Alternatives to hieroglyphic. Egyptian hieratic and demotic writing,
transcribed back into the parent script.

his death, and his sarcophagus, in true Pharaonic style, still stands in its forecourt.

The leading students of the Egyptian language in the next generation were in Germany, in particular Adolf Erman (1854–1937) and Kurt Sethe (1869–1934). Both these scholars made contributions to most branches of the Egyptian language, and Erman even succeeded in discovering an entire tense which had been missed by Champollion and everybody else. This new tense expressed states, or the results of an action, rather than the action itself, and it showed that the Egyptian language was capable of far greater subtleties than had been realised. Collectively, the work of Erman and his collaborators goes under the name of the Berlin School. Relations between members of the school may not always have been amicable (Erman, for example, complained that Sethe had 'the soul of a lawyer'), but their achievement is undeniable. They put the study of Egyptian grammar on an entirely new basis, and explored in detail the links with Semitic languages such as Hebrew and Arabic which could only be sketched by Champollion. By the end of the nineteenth century, German scholarship was far ahead of any of its rivals. In some ways, this pre-eminence has never been completely lost. Adolf Erman and his collaborators were also responsible for the great *Wörterbuch*, the many-volumed dictionary of hieroglyphs which is indispensable to anyone intending to do serious research into the Egyptian language.

In Britain the study of Egyptology tended to lag behind, and it is no coincidence that the initiative in setting up an academic post was left to an amateur, Amelia Edwards (1831–92). Edwards was one of the very first women to earn her living entirely from writing and, armed with the proceeds of her best-selling travel book *A Thousand Miles up the Nile*, she continued to browbeat for the cause. She succeeded in the face of official scepticism in creating the Egypt Exploration Society. In her will she also endowed the first chair of Egyptology in Britain, at University College London. This was more than sixty years after the Collège de France had honoured Champollion.

Amelia Edwards's greatest protégé, and the first holder of the Edwards Chair, was Flinders Petrie (1853–1942). This titanic and quarrelsome figure essentially created the modern science of archaeology, at least in the Near East. He could be at home among the colossal statues and the gold sarcophagi, but he was also one of the first to realise that anonymous and humble objects such as potsherds or fruit stones could be vital evidence as well. His invention of sequence dating, which is used to date periods such as prehistory where there are no written sources, is one of the great achievements in all archaeology. His bibliography lists over a thousand titles, including at least ninety-five books: more than one for every year of his life, together with a couple of volumes of auto-biography. The museum named after him in University College London houses 132 of his notebooks. This museum also changed the perception of archaeology in Egypt: it is a collection designed for teaching, and to introduce the student to the nature of excavating, and the evidence that can be found from this, rather than a collection devoted to works of art which are displayed and designed to provoke curios-ity and awe. This tireless archaeologist would work all day during long seasons in Egypt, often in very remote sites, and in the evening he relaxed by writing up the previous season's final report. In this he was aided by his extremely able wife, although the austerity of the couple's life in Egypt has passed into legend. Tins of corned beef would be thrown at the wall to see if they burst; if not, they were taken to be edible. A request by a visitor to be shown the toilet could be met by an ancient potsherd being pressed into the hand and a direction to the nearest sand dune. After forty years of Egypt he fell out definitively with his colleagues and started excavating in Palestine. He was knighted in 1923.

Another of the greatest names in Egyptian philology is Amelia Edwards's other protégé, Francis Llewellyn Griffith (1862–1934). Griffith was the first Egyptologist in Britain to come to terms with the discoveries of the Berlin School, and he went on to make major breakthroughs in every branch of the language. He also deciphered the Meroitic script from the Sudan, which had its own alphabet based on hieroglyphs, as well as a cursive variant derived loosely from Egyptian demotic. This decipherment of a new script using our knowledge of Egyptian hieroglyphs would have been dear to the heart of Champollion. The fact that Griffith succeeded in marrying two wealthy women in succession may have helped him to concentrate on his studies, since for much of his career, unlike Champollion, he never needed a job.

The twentieth century saw two of the most impressive scholars of the Egyptian language, particularly in the study of hieratic, which had rather trailed behind the rest of the field. Sir Alan Gardiner (1879–1963) was another man of independent means, but there are few people with this kind of leisure who can have put their time to such good use. He wrote some twenty-six books and more than 200 articles. Among these there is his *Egyptian Grammar*, which has introduced more students in the English-speaking world to the intricacies of

19. Founder of the Egypt Exploration Society and creator of the first chair of Egyptology in Britain, Amelia Edwards was also a popular writer, *c.* 1885.

the language than any other work, and which remains a best-seller after more than fifty years. His cringeworthy autobiography, on the other hand, is more likely to have the opposite effect on an aspiring Egyptologist, since it lacks any sign of the humour and self-awareness which Gardiner's friends insist that he had in abundance.

Gardiner was to work closely with a Czech who settled in England, Jaroslav Černý (1898–1970). Černý specialised in the material from Deir el Medineh, the settlement which housed the artists and workers who created the tombs in the Valley of the Kings. This material is unique in the ancient world, ranging over wills, statements of salaries and inventories of publicly funded equipment, journals, accounts of the world's first recorded strike action, literary works and a list of kings with the exact lengths of their reigns. There are also accusations against corrupt workmen and complacent authorities, and appeals to oracles to put matters right. Publication of these amazing archives has taken almost a century, and it is still continuing.

Egypt has also produced its share of Champollion's heirs, and this proportion is increasing. One of the finest Egyptian scholars of the last century was Labib Habachi (1906–84). Within his own country Habachi was the leading archaeologist of his generation, and he also pioneered the art of travelling the world to give lectures to international audiences. France, Italy, Germany, Austria, Czechoslovakia and the United States honoured him publicly. His career personifies the international fascination which Egyptology can inspire.

Hans Jacob Polotsky (1905–91) revolutionised study of the Egyptian language, and all modern work in this area reflects the fact. His knowledge of other languages is probably unique in the history of the subject, and his understanding of linguistics drove research into the twentieth century. Like all great masters, Polotsky had a wealth of disciples, some of whom reflect his breadth of knowledge and profundity. At the same time there has been a less happy tendency to theorise about the Egyptian language without wanting to come to terms with any of its details. Not all of this will help to make the ancient Egyptians live again, but there is no doubt that the study of hieroglyphs as a whole is flourishing. This is what Champollion would have wished.

North America has also made an outstanding contribution to Egyptology, starting from the second half of the nineteenth century and the growth of the great collections in New York, Brooklyn, Washington, Boston, Cleveland and Toronto. American Egyptology is characterised by its great vigour, and the attention which it gives to the discipline of art history. It has also produced two of the best writers of English prose that the subject has seen: Herbert Winlock (1884–1950) and William Hayes (1903–63). A major contribution to the growth of the subject worldwide was made by James Henry Breasted, the first American to gain a PhD in Egyptology and the inaugural director of the Oriental Institute in Chicago. *A History of Ancient Egypt* (1905), his popular masterpiece, remains one of the best introductions to Egyptology ever written. Breasted secured funds from J. D. Rockefeller, among others, both for the institute and for its second home in Luxor, Chicago House. Among its many activities is the creation of the *Chicago Demotic Dictionary*, the essential tool for anyone intending to work seriously on this phase of the language. There is also an international directory of Egyptologists working in universities or museums. According to this loose-leaf publication, the subject Champollion founded is now taught or studied in no fewer than forty-four countries. This is the true extent of Jean-François' legacy.

One of the most appealing points about Egyptian literature is that much of it was not subject to the process of sifting which took place in other cultures. In ancient Greece or Rome, and in the Christian or Islamic cultures which succeeded them, texts would be kept until they needed to be recopied. At this point, manuscripts which contained ideas which were thought to be subversive or contradicted received wisdom simply did not get transcribed, and they have vanished. The literature which we have from these cultures is censored, either for political or for ethical reasons. This applies to an extent in ancient Egypt, when it comes to state records or works of popular literature, but the sands of Egypt also preserve many other texts which would have perished in another climate. It is no accident that some of the most controversial and unorthodox books from the early history of Christianity have been found in Egypt. They may have been discarded, but they are still preserved for us to read.

In the same way, the key to understanding the hieroglyphs has given us insights into Egypt's past which are completely absent from other parts of the world. We can read a letter to the king written in demotic on a piece of potsherd. We can follow the ancient scribe as he changed his mind, wetted his thumb and erased the lines he did not like. We can even, in some cases, make out the words he erased and look at his inky thumbprint, still as fresh as when it was made. We follow ancient schoolboys as they absent-mindedly write out tenses of verbs or phrases arranged in the order of their alphabet, an order which was very different from ours. We can see the teacher's corrections in red ink, written over their pupils' fumbling attempts at grammar. We read letters that were found sealed, and become the first person after the original writer to know what they said. In this way at least, a modern student can come close to the spirit of Champollion.

We may enter into the mind of Egyptian officials as they go about their duties. In the tomb of the vizier Rekhmire, we have the chance to read the words that the king gave him on the day of his installation, thirty-five centuries ago. One piece of this royal advice seems almost postmodern in its sophistication:

> Bear in mind what was said about the vizier Akhtoy. Whenever his friends or family petitioned him about a matter, he always found against them, for fear of people saying, 'He favours his own'. That is excess of justice.

There is the timeless world of the romantic tales, such as *The Two Brothers* and *The Doomed Prince*. In stories such as these the cows talk, and the prince's faithful dog talks too. There is a princess living at the top of a tower who could have come out of one of Grimm's fairy tales, and a water demon and a crocodile do battle with each other daily in the lake. The wife of the elder brother pretends that the younger brother has seduced her, and as a result the younger brother is threatened with his life and banished. This motif is ages old, and it recurs in the biblical story of Joseph and the Greek myth of Hippolytus and Phaedra. Such profound human themes are too good to waste, and they are recycled and reshaped from one culture and language to another. Fate stalks these idylls and sets out to destroy the peace of family life. Even the prince's dog turns menacing at one point, but we do not have the end of this particular tale, and it may be that things will turn out well for the enchanted hero after all.

We are also fortunate to have one of the most remarkable stories to survive from antiquity. *The Voyage of Wenamun* is known from a single copy, now in Moscow. The manuscript dates from around 1100 BC. The tale begins like a factual report of a mission into what is now Lebanon, to acquire cedar logs for the state barge of the god Amun at Thebes. However, this is soon overlaid by a series of adventures which could almost have come out of Homer's *Odyssey*: the arrival of pirates looking for the hero, who has been stranded for twenty-nine days in the harbour at Byblos, and a detour to Cyprus, where Wenamun is washed up on the shore before the queen of the island, who happens to be on her way from one of her palaces to the other one. It includes moments which could have come out of the early nineteenth-century Romantic movement, such as this account of Wenamun's first meeting with the ruler of Byblos:

> *He took me up, while the [statue of] the god was resting in its tent by the shore of the sea. I found the ruler sitting in his upper room, with his back turned to a window, and the waves of the great Syrian sea were beating behind his head.*

Then there is the reply of the same ruler to a monologue about civilisation which Wenamun has given him as a substitute for ready cash:

Amun thunders in the sky, but only when he has placed the storm god there beside him. And Amun created all the lands of the earth, but only after he had created the land of Egypt, where you came from the other day. And culture came from there to end up in the place where I am, and wisdom likewise. So why these pointless journeyings which you are busy with?

Finally, here is Wenamun at his most desolate, by the shore of the Syrian sea:

I sat there weeping. And the scribe of the ruler came out and asked, 'What is the matter?' I said to him, 'Can't you see the wading birds who are returning for a second time to Egypt? Look at them; they are heading for the cool pools. How long shall I be here, abandoned?

It is worth learning Late Egyptian for this story alone.

An earlier tale, *The Man Who Was Tired of Life*, is also known from a single text, which suggests that it never achieved much popularity. Most of this tale takes the form of a dialogue between a man and his soul, ranging over themes such as the desire for suicide, death as a homecoming, the meaning of life in a world without trust, and the question of whether a woman who dies after experiencing life is more to be pitied than her children who 'looked upon the face of the crocodile before they lived'. This work anticipates Freud, and some twentieth-century literature, by as much as 4,000 years.

Some things are more homely, but equally moving. There is the short song, like a nursery rhyme, inscribed above a scene of threshing on the wall of the tomb of Paheri at El

Kab, south of Luxor, which so captivated Champollion when he first read it:

> Thresh for yourselves, oxen; thresh for yourselves; thresh
> for yourselves.
> The straw for yourselves; the corn for your masters.

There is also the lament for a drowned shepherd which is inscribed on one of the walls of an Old Kingdom tomb from Saqqara, above a scene showing rams treading in the earth after the flood has receded, and cows being tempted across a stream by a farmer carrying one of their calves in front of them. This dates from before 2300 BC, and may be the oldest song in the world:

> *Where is the shepherd, the shepherd of the West? The shepherd is
> in the water among the fish; he chatters with the catfish, and rubs
> noses with the nose-fish in the West. Where is the shepherd, the
> shepherd of the West?*

In the museum in Turin there is an illustrated papyrus showing a man and a woman enjoying an inventive range of erotic activities, accompanied by the hieratic equivalent of speech bubbles. These would probably be hilarious if we understood them, but they seem to be full of local allusions and hidden meanings. The man has the shaven head of a priest, whereas the woman is far more earthy, and pays constant attention to her make-up, even when we would expect her to be otherwise distracted. We are obviously dealing with the ancient equivalent of the actress and the bishop. The opening part of the papyrus is devoted to pictures of animal

20. The ancient equivalents of the actress and the bishop in conversation,
as depicted on a papyrus in Turin.

fables. Anyone asking what this well-thumbed papyrus roll contained could be reassured by being shown the first few pictures. '*What* have you got there?' 'Animal fables, dear.'

Texts such as *Wenamun*, and for all we know the actress and the bishop, were designed to last, and they could be copied and recopied. But the dry climate of Egypt also preserves things which were intended to be short-lived, such as tax receipts, shopping lists and business memoranda. These are the verbal equivalents of snapshots, rather than formal portrait groups. The mayor of Thebes in about 1425 BC was a man named Sennufer, who had started his career as a temple gardener. His tomb on the west bank at Luxor is a popular sight for tourists, who are attracted by the vines which are painted so naturalistically over the ceiling. This could have been all there is to be known about Sennufer, and we could count ourselves lucky even if we only had his colourful tomb. But a letter of his also survives, a chance find from somewhere nearby. It is a message to one of his employees:

> *The mayor of the southern capital Sennufer speaks to the tenant-farmer Baki son of Kyson, to the following effect. This letter is brought to you to tell you that I am coming to see you when we moor at Hu in three days' time. Do not let me find fault with you in your duties. Do not fail to have things in perfect order. Also, pick for me numerous plants, lotuses and flowers, and others worth offering. Further, you are to cut 5,000 boards and 200 timbers; then the boat which will bring me can carry them, since you have not cut any wood this year – understood? On no account be slack. If you are not able to cut them you should approach Woser, the mayor of Hu. Pay attention: the herdsman of Cusae and the cowherds who are under my authority, fetch them*

*for yourself in order to cut the wood, along with the workmen
who are with you. Also, you are to order the herdsmen to prepare
milk in new jars in anticipation of my arrival – understood?
You are not to slack, because I know that you are a* wiwi, *and
fond of eating in bed.*

Hu and Cusae are towns on the river to the north of Thebes.
The precise meaning of the Egyptian word *wiwi* is unknown,
but it is clear that Sennufer suspects that his tenant is inef-
fectual in some way. The letter was intended to dismay poor
Baki and spur him to action, but it is something of a relief to
discover that he never read it. The papyrus on which it was
written was found rolled up and sealed, as it was when it was
sent almost 3,500 years ago. The Egyptologist who published
this letter was the first person ever to read it, and thanks to
this chance discovery we are in a position to eavesdrop upon
the past. Some of the thrill that Champollion found when he
started to make sense of the ancient words can be felt when
we read this ephemeral letter.

There are more refined sentiments in some of the various
love poems which have come down to us, most of them
dating to what is known as the Ramesside period in the thir-
teenth and twelfth centuries BC. Here, lovers find themselves
locked out of their girlfriends' houses and are reduced to ser-
enading the door bolts. Others wish they were items of their
loved one's jewellery or clothing, so that she could hold them
close to her. Girls wade into the water in their wet robes and
invite their admirers to gaze at the fish in their hands. Figs
and pomegranates grow to ripeness in their gardens in the
heat of the afternoon. Champollion, who wrote love poems
of his own, would have appreciated these songs. One of the

mysteries of Egyptology is that poems which are uncannily similar to these Ramesside examples are found almost a thousand years later in Alexandria, this time written in Greek by poets such as Theocritus and Callimachus. There must be a link between the two traditions, since the resemblances are so striking, but so far no one has come up with an explanation.

What she has done to me, the sister [i.e. sweetheart], how
can I keep it silent?
Leaving me at the entrance to her house, going into her
home alone!
Not even wishing me safe return, so taking away my night
from me!
I passed by the house of my sweetheart in the dark;
I knocked, and nobody opened to me. 'Good night' to the
porter.
Bolt, I will open you. Door, you are my guiding destiny,
you are my kindly fate.

Another mystery of Egyptology is the tomb known as number 55 in the Valley of the Kings. Inside there was a badly damaged coffin, originally designed for a woman but refashioned to contain the body of a man. Many books and articles have been devoted to who that man was, and whose tomb, and whose coffin, he ended up in. Scholars have spent whole careers thinking about this puzzle, but it seems increasingly likely that the original owner of the gilded coffin in Tomb 55 was a lady named Kiya. This princess is a shadowy figure, but she is known to be the minor wife of the revolutionary Pharaoh Akhenaten, who was also married to the more famous Nefertiti. Kiya may also turn out to be the mother of

Tutankhamun. Here is the reconstructed text from the base of her coffin, in which she envisages the prospect of eternity in the presence of her husband and the new god whom he worshipped, the Aten, the emblem of the sun. Tomb 55 was not discovered until seventy years after the death of Champollion, but he would have delighted in the words which the lady Kiya chose for her afterlife:

> *Words spoken by [the princess Kiya], justified. I will breathe the sweet breath which comes forth from your lips, I will behold your beauty every day. My prayer is to hear your voice, sweet like the north breeze. Your limbs will be young in life, through my love of you, and you will give me your arms which bear your spirit. I will receive it, and live through it. You will call out my name for eternity, and it will never fail on your lips. My [lord Akhenaten], you abide for ever and ever, alive like the Aten … King of Upper and Lower Egypt who lives upon truth, lord of the Two Lands, the beautiful child of the living Aten who is here, alive for ever and ever.*

These are a few of the voices which Champollion and his heirs have enabled us to hear again.

8

THE WORDS OF THE STONE

[King Ptolemy] has created temples, shrines and altars once more
for the gods; he has put other things in order, since he is at heart
a god pious towards the gods. He has sought after the glories of
the temples, to make them new again in his time as Pharaoh, as
is fitting. In exchange for this the gods have granted him might,
victory and triumph, prosperity and health; and all other bless-
ings for his reign as Pharaoh are secured for him, together with
his children.

Rosetta Stone, demotic version, lines 20–21

The Rosetta Stone has proved to be the key to the glories of
Egyptian literature, but what role does it play itself in that
literature? It has given us the cast list, and whatever remains
of the original drama, but does it deserve a part in the play?
Strictly speaking, the stone is a historical record, and not a
work of imaginative writing, but the term literature is often
used in a catch-all sense by Egyptologists, and many, if not
all, historical records turn out on close inspection to have an
element of fiction in them. Seen in this light, the stone can
qualify as a work of literature.

The text of the stone gives the terms of an agreement
drawn up by a synod of Egyptian priests which had gathered

in Memphis, the city which had been the religious capital of the country for much of its history. This took place on 27 March 196 BC, the day after the anniversary of the king's coronation. The other party to this agreement was the king himself, the Macedonian ruler of Egypt, Ptolemy V, who took the surname Epiphanes, Greek for 'god manifest'. Other copies of this agreement are known, and the master text is normally referred to as the Decree of Memphis. Ptolemy, the founder of the dynasty, had been one of Alexander the Great's generals. He realised the importance of Egypt as a power base against his rivals and seized control of the place after Alexander's death. The strategy proved so successful that Ptolemy turned out to be the only one of Alexander's generals to die in his own bed rather than on the battlefield. The first four Ptolemies were impressive figures, and Ptolemy V had more than a century of glory to look back upon. Much of that glory was associated with the new foundation of Alexandria, which had become the political and cultural capital of the Hellenistic state, not to mention the leading city in the Greek world. Ptolemy Epiphanes came to the throne at an early age, and when the text of the stone was drawn up he was still only fourteen. What is known of the rest of his reign, however, shows that he is the first Ptolemy to whom we can safely apply the adjective nondescript.

The text of the stone, on the other hand, is at pains to portray this youthful ruler as the latest manifestation of the ideal Pharaoh. As befits a statement drawn up by the highest clergy in the land, the flattery begins with an account of the generosity that the king has shown towards the temples of Egypt, showering them with wealth in the form of money and grain supplies. He has rewarded his

21. Radiant mediocrity: a coin of Ptolemy V Epiphanes,
hero of the Rosetta Stone.

troops, as well a youthful and inexperienced ruler might. He has cut taxes, and other dues which were payable to the crown. The building of Alexandria was now complete, and the great library and the Pharos lighthouse had become the glories of the new Egypt and its glittering capital. The royal house was still extremely prosperous, so these popular concessions could be afforded. In addition, there has been an amnesty for prisoners, some of them after serving very lengthy sentences indeed. The generous Pharaoh has continued the state subsidy to the temples which had been paid by his father, Ptolemy IV Philopator. The fees required from priests on taking up their offices (essentially a tax hidden under a euphemism) have also been remitted. A quaint detail follows, which would have intrigued Nelson: the press gang for sailors has been abolished.

The years immediately before the synod of Memphis had been violent, and the text of the stone does not trouble to disguise this. A revolt had broken out in the middle of the Delta, centred on the town of Shekan, or Lycopolis ('Wolf-town') in the Greek. The city fell, but only after the surrounding canals had been blocked. This reminds us of the situation around French-occupied Alexandria during the British blockade in 1801, although there the British resorted to the opposite tactic of flooding the hinterland. The ringleaders of the uprising, who are represented as the nadir of godless ingratitude, were put to death on the stake. But the stone was intended to cast a positive light on events, and the point is clearly made that others who had been involved in the revolt were promptly pardoned. More temple payments to the crown are now remitted, and there is also a lengthy section describing the piety of the king towards two sacred bulls named Apis and Mnevis. Rather like an animal equivalent of the Dalai Lama, these bulls were calves who had been chosen by the priesthood on the basis of birthmarks. They were believed to be the re-embodiments of their predecessors, and they were credited with being oracles who were in touch with divine wisdom. On their deaths they were given state funerals and returned to the gods, whereupon the priests once again travelled the land, looking for their successors. Piety towards animals like these, even on the part of a Greek-speaking newcomer, was a sure way to secure the loyalty of many thousands of native Egyptians. As a result of all this, the stone confirms that the king is fit to be compared to Thoth the twice-great, the god of learning and civilisation, and he is also the very image of Horus, the son and champion of Isis and Osiris.

What did the synod of priests concede as a return for all this generosity? A run of statues of the king was to be commissioned, showing the god of the respective temple offering him the sword of victory. A copy was to be placed 'in the temple, in each and every temple, and in the principal place within the temple'. Other statues of the king are to be kept in the holy of holies of the sacred places, along with the images of the gods worshipped there. The shrine containing the king's image is to be adorned with ten golden crowns, each one accompanied by a uraeus, the divine cobra which was the emblem of Pharaonic kingship. Private individuals are to be encouraged to install duplicates of these shrines in their homes, in order to demonstrate their loyalty to the crown. The anniversaries of the king's birthday and his coronation are to be major festivals from this day henceforth, celebrated with processions and garlands. All priests are to become priests of Ptolemy Epiphanes, in addition to the gods whom they happen to serve, and hieroglyphs to this effect are to be engraved on their rings of office. Finally, the contents of the synod's decree are to be set down in hieroglyphs ('the writing of the divine words'), demotic ('the writing of documents') and Greek ('the writing of the Ionians'), and a copy of the text is to be placed in every temple of the first, second and third division in the land. It was this last clause, glimpsed in the Greek version of the stone, which alerted the French savants to its importance.

These acts sound grandiose, and there is no doubt that all these statues, garlands and gilded crowns cost money, but it is difficult not to come away from this text with the feeling that the real concessions in this ritual bargain have been made by the king, even while his piety and generosity are being trumpeted to all. The tax breaks and amnesties given by the crown to the temples must have greatly outweighed the cost of mass-producing shrines with crowns on them. Why has Ptolemy Epiphanes allowed himself to be manoeuvred into this expensive and unequal deal with the priesthood of a land he was supposed to control?

The short answer is that the priesthood of the Egyptian temples were in a position to deliver loyalty. They were not only the clergy of their day, but also what Marx would have termed the intelligentsia. The gods of the Egyptians exerted a powerful fascination over the minds of the Pharaoh's subjects, and the Pharaoh himself was part of that mystique, even if that office was currently occupied by someone of Macedonian descent who could not read a hieroglyph. Temples were also major employers and wealthy landowners, with control over activities such as linen manufacture and metalwork. Many of these land holdings and wealth-creating industries paid taxes to the crown, and it was these taxes which provided for the army, together with much of the rest of the Ptolemaic state. If the priesthood of these influential bodies could be kept on side, a good part of the Pharaoh's work would be done for him. The temples, with their alien rituals and hieroglyphic hot air, were necessary to keep the Egyptians where Ptolemy needed them to be.

This would have been true of any earlier Pharaoh, and it was true of the first four Ptolemies as well. The third century BC in Egypt, and particularly in Alexandria, had been one of prosperity, and a glory that was thought to be inexhaustible. But this was turning out to be finite too, and the strength of

22. A priest of Ptolemaic Egypt. Head of a statue in the Brooklyn Museum.

the Ptolemaic kingdom was beginning to decline. One way of measuring this is to look at the series of wars which the Ptolemies fought against their Hellenistic neighbours, the Seleucid kings who controlled Syria and Palestine, and who traced their ancestry back to another of Alexander's warring generals. These too were part of the original empire of Alexander the Great, but there was nothing the Greeks liked more than fighting each other, and now they were able to do this on something nearer to a global scale. In the first three wars which Egypt fought with the Seleucids, the Ptolemies were more than able to hold their own, and on several occasions they succeeded in carrying the war back into enemy territory. At one point they even seized control of the port of the Seleucid capital, Syrian Antioch.

Things went differently, however, when it came to the fourth Syrian War. Here the Ptolemies achieved some successes, but the decisive point came on 22 June 217 BC, a mere twenty-one years before the Rosetta Stone was composed. The two armies met at Raphia, which is nowadays in the Gaza Strip. Both sides fielded about 70,000 men, but Hellenistic armies also used elephants in war, partly because of their strength, but also because the smell of them could terrify cavalry horses. Ptolemy IV had seventy-three elephants of war at his command; the Seleucid king had 102. The Pharaoh himself rode out into the heart of the battlefield, the last ancient Egyptian ruler to do so in Asia. The Egyptian elephants turned and charged back into their own ranks, and the left flank of the Ptolemaic army was routed by the Seleucids. It looked as if the battle was lost. What spared Ptolemy IV was his right flank, and it was here that the majority of his native Egyptians were stationed. The Seleucid nerve finally broke, and Raphia, contrary to all expectations, turned into a Ptolemaic victory. We will never know to what extent the Egyptian soldiery really saved the day at Raphia, but the point is that this is what the Egyptians believed, and so did many of the Greeks who had fought with them. The despised peasant, with his diet of onions and his crocodile-headed gods, had a value after all: he had protected Ptolemaic Egypt from invasion.

Another change was at work in Egypt as the third century BC gave way to the second, and this was the nature of the population itself. After Alexander had conquered the country, immigrants from all over the Greek world flooded into Egypt, in search of opportunities in a land which was potentially extremely wealthy. The Ptolemies were the richest family on earth, and they were known to be generous employers. The result was the single biggest migration that the country has known, even in its dynasty-long history. But most of these new migrants were men, and not all of them were content to hang around street corners in the Greek-style cities. Many of them were ambitious to work the land, and for this they would need wives and children, as well as native servants or employees. These Greeks married Egyptian women, who had a reputation for seductive ways and slinky cosmetics. No matter how much classical education was spent on their children in the gymnasia schools, they were going to be half Egyptian, and the third and fourth generations of their offspring were bound gradually to feel that they were less and less Greek. There was also the fact that Greek families seem to have had a preference for male children, and newborn girls were frequently left to die in the streets. Egyptian families, where the sexes enjoyed more equality and another pair of hands was always useful, were in the habit of picking up these children. These girls would become Egyptian too. The question of who was a Greek and who was an Egyptian under Ptolemaic rule was starting to be a tricky one. The chattering classes were changing: they were now talking more and more in demotic Egyptian as well as in the previously dominant Greek.

It is no coincidence that immediately after the Battle of Raphia an Egyptian revolt began. A large number of Egyptians had been drafted into the Ptolemaic army, and they will have returned with many of their prejudices confirmed. Ptolemaic courtiers were irresponsibly wealthy and frequently corrupt, and at Raphia the officer class had come close to ruining everything for Greek and Egyptian alike. Some of these Egyptian soldiers returned to rural poverty, and took to hiding out on the fringes of the deserts, where they could lead more profitable lives as smugglers and outlaws. Growing Egyptian self-confidence and suspicion of Alexandria and all its ways meant that many of these rebels would find support and protection among their fellow countrymen in the 20,000 villages which, according to the historian Herodotus, made up the bulk of the population.

The revolt began in the north of the country, in the Delta. This was close to Alexandria, and Ptolemaic forces were always on hand to try to suppress it. Communications in the Delta are complicated, since the region is criss-crossed with canals and roads which can become submerged. This created never-ending problems for the government, but it also meant that the rebels had difficulty in combining their forces. The result was a stalemate which lasted for thirty years after Raphia. It is one of the skirmishes in this long struggle, the revolt at Lycopolis, in the centre of the Delta, which is described on the Rosetta Stone. This state of affairs dragged on until 185 BC, when Ptolemy Epiphanes issued the ringleaders a fake amnesty, then put them to death when they trustingly arrived for talks.

The situation in the south of the country was more serious. Here the Nile valley forms a continuous ribbon of land between two deserts, and travel along the river was straightforward for most of the time. The rebels succeeded in taking over a whole swathe of Upper Egypt, and were able to declare unilateral independence. In 206 BC one of their number, who bore the Egyptian name Haronnophris, was proclaimed the rightful Pharaoh, and legal documents are known which are dated by the years of his reign. The capital of the south, the splendid city of Thebes, soon fell under rebel control. Haronnophris was then succeeded by a man named Anchonnophris, whose name suggests he was either a relative or a devoted imitator. (Until recently these names were thought to read Harmachis and Anchmachis, but it is reassuring to know that Egyptology moves on. People's careers can hinge on improvements like these. Where Egyptian is concerned, we are still deciphering.) The rebels were able to recruit soldiers from Nubia, an area where Ptolemaic rule had often been shaky. The government garrisons in Upper Egypt either surrendered or fled to the north. This stand-off between the government forces in Lower and Middle Egypt and the breakaway Pharaohs in the south lasted for twenty years, until 186 BC, when a major victory by the Ptolemaic general Komanos put an end to the matter. In the first part of his reign, Ptolemy V was fortunate in his advisers, and he was also blessed with at least one outstanding general.

What this means is that the Ptolemy V Epiphanes who is

the star of the Rosetta Stone was the ruler of Egypt in name only. A sizeable part of the country was outside his control, and this was a situation which could well get worse. This Greek-speaking king needed the native temples, far more than he needed pliant courtiers or elephants who could turn and rend. He had no choice but to reach for the temples' wealth, and their hold over the minds of his subjects. Without these, he might lose control of everywhere outside Alexandria and a few outposts in the Greek world. The house of Ptolemy could fall, particularly with a fourteen-year-old boy in charge of it. In that case, what would become of those Egyptians, such as the members of the synod of Memphis, who had collaborated with that house? This is what the Rosetta Stone is telling us, in the midst of the shrines and floral bouquets and re-engraved rings on the fingers of the priests. We are in a position to know the outcome of the revolt of the Thebaid, but the scribes who drew up the text of the Rosetta Stone were not. They were living in critical times, and this is why the Pharaoh and the native priesthood needed to do their unequal deal.

This is what the Rosetta inscription has to tell us about ancient history, and what it says is important enough. But the stone as a source for that history is not uniquely important, and compared with many other texts which have survived from Egypt its contribution is minor. There are other copies of the Decree of Memphis in existence, and there are other edicts from other synods which are equally valuable to scholarship. The argument is sometimes heard that the rightful place for the Rosetta Stone is back in Egypt, because it was created there and is a part of the history of that country. There is something in this argument, but to answer it in full we will need to fall back on an old objection which can sound pedantic, although it is sometimes unavoidable: it depends on what you mean by history.

The German language has two words for 'history', and it would be helpful if English did too. One of these, *Geschichte*, refers to the events of history, together with their causes and the sequences into which they fall. The other, *Historie*, is applied to the narrative which we choose to weave round these events, and also to the philosophy and assumptions which we bring to understanding them. There is a difference, after all, between thinking about ancient Egyptian history and writing *a history* of ancient Egypt. In terms of the first type of history, there is no doubt that the Rosetta Stone has a part to play, although it is not a part in the first division: instead, it has to be content with a supporting role. What it does is to give us an episode in the *Geschichte* of its original homeland.

When it comes to the second concept of history, the stone's role is very different. It is the creator of the entire *Historie* of ancient Egypt, because it has enabled us to read the texts which led us to start writing that history. In this second story it is the starring player; it may even be that there are no other players, and the play is really a monologue. The home of the events the stone describes is Egypt. But where is the homeland of the play, the entire drama which it has brought into being? The real impact of the Rosetta Stone has been not on the ancient world, where it originated, but on the modern world, to which it migrated in 1802. Its contribution to our international understanding of that history is what makes the stone unique. Learning French was perhaps the best thing the stone ever did. It enabled us to recreate its past, and to make that past an element in our present.

9

....

WHOSE LOOT IS IT ANYWAY?

What are the hopes of man? Old Egypt's King
Cheops erected the first pyramid
And largest, thinking it was just the thing
To keep his memory whole and mummy hid;
But somebody or other rummaging,
Burglariously broke his coffin's lid:
Let not a monument give you or me hopes,
Since not a pinch of dust remains of Cheops.

Lord Byron, lines added as an afterthought to *Don Juan* (1819)

Indeed, had the monuments nothing to fear but the water and
the seasons, they might exist for ages, but they have to encounter
the violence of the Turks … and yet more, the hands of certain
Europeans. I shall mention no names, but merely observe that
they are not French …

introduction to catalogue by Frédéric Caillaud (who was French) (1822)

The stone may have given us Egypt's past, but it can also be a source of strife. In the second chapter of this book it was explained how animosity broke out between the English and the French military immediately after it was discovered. This rivalry later migrated to the camps of scholarship, with supporters of Thomas Young trying to undermine the claims that were being made across the Channel for Champollion. Even now, the question of where the stone rightly belongs continues to surface. From time to time articles appear in the Egyptian press, questioning the right of the British Museum to claim it as its own. Some of these articles are linked to other causes, such as a campaign to build a new Egyptian museum or a similar prestige project. The Egyptian government has put in a diplomatic request to have the stone returned, but they have not contacted the British Museum directly about this. But this may change, and the question is one that we ought to think about. To do this, it will help if we turn away from the stone for a little and look at the wider picture.

The best-known claim for repatriation is of course the campaign to bring the Elgin Marbles back to Athens. There are legal aspects to this, but the case that reaches the public tends to be an emotional one, which depends heavily on the notion of the Glory that was Greece and the feeling that the Parthenon sculptures were designed to rest under the blue skies of Attica, inhaling the stimulating pines, and not under the rain of London, breathing in the smog. At the least, the campaign to restore the marbles can give a *raison d'être* to ageing actors or politicians, since it helps to keep their names before the public. Some major figures in the academic world outside Greece are known to favour the marbles' return. It is very difficult not to sympathise with a cause like this, which appealed so strongly to Elgin's contemporary Lord Byron. But what does it imply for the rest of the world's collecting habits?

What happens if we start to reverse the history of acquisition? How many chances of events or quirks of human nature will need to be righted if we are to do justice all round? The United States is full of paintings, furniture and manuscripts which were created in Britain. Should these be returned to British skies and the scent of English hay? No doubt these treasures were acquired legally, but would they be given export licences today? Should the law of this particular day take precedence over the values of yesterday? In general we do not take kindly to the idea that human beings should be returned to their places of origin, in spite of the fact that their homelands might have a moral claim on their talents. This applies especially when the newcomers have made honest efforts to build up a new life. What about the Rosetta Stone, which has similarly found a new home, and perhaps even a new life? If a piece of granite had rights, what would these rights be? If it has no rights, what does this tell us about our responsibilities towards it?

Some while ago there was an exhibition in London devoted to some of the finest animal sculptures ever made, the bronze horses which used to stand on the façade of St Mark's in Venice. These horses have been in Venice ever since 1204, so we can argue that they have found a home there. But they were looted by the Venetians from Constantinople, as part of the breakaway crusade which Venice financed and which led to the sacking of the greatest city in Christendom. This was a distinctly shameful affair, which has never been forgotten by the Orthodox Church. Does this mean that the horses should be sent back to Istanbul, the city that Constantinople has become?

The horses were created not in Constantinople, but more likely somewhere in the Greek or Hellenistic world. So do they belong in some part of Greece? The Genoese tried to grab them off the Venetians, but failed. Napoleon took a shining to them and carted them off to Paris in 1797, two years before his officers discovered the Rosetta Stone. In Paris they were probably more accessible to scholars, but does this accessibility amount to a claim that they were better off in Paris, and should be put back there? The outcome of Waterloo restored the statues to Venice. Does a battle, which was determined by force of arms and in all likelihood the weather too, have the right to be an arbiter of things like this? Who owns these horses, and who should own them?

Constantinople, properly known as New Rome, was designed to be one of the treasure-houses of the world. The emperor Constantine and his successors went out of their way to cram the place with relics of paganism and Christianity alike. In the hippodrome there stands an Egyptian obelisk, similar to the ones which have made their way to Rome. Under the great column in the forum there were nails of the Crucifixion and fragments of the True Cross, which had been recovered by Constantine's mother, Helena, the most successful archaeologist in history, at least to judge from the stories about her. The mysterious portrait of Jesus known as the Mandylion found its way there from Edessa in south-east Turkey. None of these items was native to Constantinople.

Also in the hippodrome there is a bronze column, surmounted by a golden tripod. This object was earlier set up in the courtyard of the great church of Hagia Sophia, whence it was later transferred. This too was an immigrant. The column was described by the patron of all tourist guides, the writer Pausanias, in the second century AD. He saw it on the Sacred Way in Apollo's holy city of Delphi, in north-central Greece. According to his account, which there is no reason

23. Obelisks and remains of the tripod from Delphi in the hippodrome at Constantinople, photograph *c.* 1890.

to doubt, the tripod and the column, which took the form of three serpents intertwined, was a dedication to the god of Delphi by another Pausanias, the general of the confederacy which won the final victory over the invading Persians. This was the Battle of Plataea, in 479 BC. A Greek claim to ownership of this object must surely be very strong. But the bronze itself was melted down from the spoils of the defeated Persian army. The odds are that the metal of which this column is cast is of Iranian origin. Should the serpent column be presented to the Islamic Republic as a gesture of reconciliation and solidarity?

Another object in Istanbul is the so-called Alexander sarcophagus, where it is one of the many treasures of the Archaeological Museum. In spite of its name, this is not the resting place of the great conqueror, who was buried in Egypt. It is carved with exquisite scenes of Alexander and his companion Hephaestion hunting, and it was found in the royal necropolis at Sidon, on the coast of what is now Lebanon. It may have been intended for a man named Abdalonymos, who was plucked from his gardening job by Alexander and told to rule the city for him while he went on to conquer the rest of the Persian Empire. Should the Lebanese government be putting in a claim for this masterpiece, or does it belong in one of the places that identify themselves with Macedonia, the home of the Alexander without whom the sarcophagus would never have been made in the first place? One empire in the making created the Alexander sarcophagus, and another, the Ottoman, was responsible for moving it to Istanbul. Which empire is supposed to win out, in a case like this?

The horses of St Mark's are still in Venice, inside the

24. The other Cleopatra's Needle, awaiting transport from
Alexandria to New York, 1880.

basilica (the ones outside are replicas), but this only serves to remind us that this building can be culturally dubious as well. It is erected over the resting place of the remains of the Apostle who gave his name to the second of the four Gospels. St Mark can be regarded as a Venetian by adoption, and his emblem, the lion, can be seen all over the city where he now lies. But he was originally buried in Alexandria in Egypt, and he is still the patron saint of that country. Surely he is as much a part of the history of Egypt as the Rosetta Stone is, and perhaps more so? The saint rested in peace for the greater part of a millennium in Alexandria in another basilica, but the city began to fall on meaner days. In the year 829 two Venetian adventurers succeeded in acquiring the body of Mark from his impoverished guardians, and they proceeded to smuggle him out through customs in a barrel, declaring on oath that he was pickled pork and offering to pay the appropriate rate of duty. The body of St Mark is in Venice today only as a result of this deception. Perhaps he should be returned to the country where he devoted so much of his life to spreading the new faith. There are elements in the Catholic Church who seem to agree with this; at any rate, some small parts which are thought to belong to his body have been returned to the Coptic authorities in Egypt, as a sort of token. We can agree that this is a start, but what about the rest of him?

St Mark died in Egypt, but it is equally important to remember where he was born. According to tradition, he came from one of the wealthier families in first-century Jerusalem, and a spacious room in his family house was the one used for the Last Supper. He was a Jew, and therefore in theory the Israeli authorities might have an interest in him. However, he did go on to become a Christian, so this is one act of repatriation which may not take place. But what if DNA analysis moves on to the point where we can identify living relatives, among either the modern Israelis or the Palestinians? Would these claims of flesh and blood be allowed to outweigh the sentiments of religion, Coptic, Orthodox or Catholic?

With the coming of Christianity to Alexandria, St Mark took the place of Alexander the Great, who had enjoyed the honour of being corpse-in-residence in that city during the centuries of pagan rule. From time to time the story surfaces that the priests who sold the body of their saint to the Venetian traders could not bring themselves to part with the Apostle who had been the companion of St Peter and St Paul. Instead, they substituted the body of Alexander, a discredited megalomaniac whose day had long since passed. What if the remains underneath St Mark's should turn out to be the great Alexander in person? It is perhaps every schoolboy archaeologist's dream to find this greatest of all conquerors. In adult reality, the result would be a cacophony of focus groups, and a politically correct nightmare. All sorts of countries would lay claim to him, and politicians would fight proxy wars using his name. Whole continents would want him, since he was born in Europe, died in Asia and was buried in Africa, that is if he is not in Venice. Like a certain breed of cat, Alexander had one eye a shade of blue and the other greenish brown, a condition which is known to medical experts as *heterochromia iridium*. Organisations defending the rights of people who are born with eyes of a different colour, or mothers who play with snakes as part of their religion, would immediately number him as one of their own and make demands accordingly. Somebody would then point out that the Greek kingdoms which he founded in the east were responsible for dragging the Romans into the Mediterranean and setting up an even bigger empire there. People would start making formal apologies for their ancestors' wrongdoings, and claims for reparations would probably follow, addressed to the governments of Italy and both the Macedonias.

With luck this will remain a harmless fantasy, but there is enough absurdity in the real world to make us worry about our sanity. The Treasure of Priam is the name given to a collection of jewellery and other objects found by the German archaeologist and adventurer Heinrich Schliemann (1822–90) at some point around the year 1873. According to the excavator, the treasures came from the site of Troy, where he had been working. Whatever the truth about this, there is no doubt that most of the find passed into Schliemann's possession. It was given by him to the German people in 1880, with the intention that it should be housed in Berlin, the capital of the newly unified state. There the treasure remained until 1945, when it disappeared amid the chaos at the end of the Second World War. Its whereabouts, if it even had one, remained unknown until 1994, when it was revealed that the objects had been for the previous forty years in Russia, most of them in the Pushkin Museum in Moscow.

Several countries soon put in claims to the Trojan treasure. One was Germany, on the understandable grounds that the objects had been in Berlin and had been acquired from the owner legally. Another was Russia, on the basis that it had them by right of conquest, and anyway it was entitled to reparation for the damage that their own works of art had suffered during the war. The third was Turkey, which argued that Troy was situated squarely within that country, and the original ownership of the finds had been disputed; in addition, the Turkish state was now in a position to devote the care to their preservation that such masterpieces deserved. An extra complication was provided by the heirs of Schliemann's business partner, Frank Calvert, who had bought part of the site of Troy. His descendants might well be entitled to a share in the finds which came from there. There were even rumours that the Greeks were thinking of putting in a claim to the treasure, possibly because Homer, who put Troy on the map, had written in Greek, and Schliemann's wife had also come from Greece. As far as I know, this claim never materialised, which is just as well, since it could have undermined the same country's claim to objects, such as the Elgin Marbles, which had been taken from there. The wrangles over Priam and his treasure still continue. This may benefit the lawyers, but it does nothing for the archaeologists.

How easily the moral high ground can shift from one peak to another. There is even a murky side to the Parthenon which is not often explored. After the Persians left the Greek mainland in 479 BC, there was no certainty that they had gone for good. Under the prompting of the Athenians, a league was formed, comprising many of the islands in the Aegean and the ports surrounding that sea. The headquarters of this league was the sacrosanct island of Delos, and its treasury was also to be situated there. It was not long before Athens started leaning on its smaller allies to move that treasury. The threat was too great. The new headquarters turned out to be the Acropolis of Athens, but the threat which was so great was no longer from the Persians; it was now from the big brother himself. Some of the Parthenon was built from money appropriated from the Delian League, and the famous Elgin Marbles are, in a sense, the product of a protection racket. Should the other islands who helped pay for the treasures of the Acropolis be compensated after all this time for the injustice which was done to them by their Athenian protectors?

If there are injustices between nations, there can also be inequalities within the same nations. There are calls from time to time to repatriate the Lewis chessmen from the British Museum to the more bracing climate of the Hebrides or somewhere else in Scotland. On the Greek island of Lemnos there is a charming museum. It was on this island in 1885 that an inscription was discovered which has turned out to be related to Etruscan, the great mystery language of ancient Italy. On a visit to the island I was keen to see this inscription, which I imagined would be in the museum there. When I could not find it, I asked an assistant. The assistant looked wistful and told me in hushed tones of regret that it was in Athens. They wanted it back on Lemnos, and it would be quite safe there. Where does this inscription belong: in a city which happens to be a European capital or in the microclimate of its original home? Can the people of modern Tuscany also make a claim to it, on the grounds that it contains the language of their ancestors?

Whole nations can lose their cultural heritage through no fault of their own. The modern state of Bangladesh used to be part of British India, and as a result many of its treasures went to Calcutta, or later New Delhi. Then it became East Pakistan, and yet more valuable objects found their way to the western part of this divided country. Now it is an independent state, but none of these treasures has been returned.

What claims does this poor country have on its neighbours? How should it be compensated, and by whom?

The truth is that the whole question of who owns what can turn into something surreal. An extreme case of this is shown in the saga of Kennewick Man, who everyone agrees is a very early American. The bones of this man were found in Washington State, in the summer of 1996. The skull appeared European, and at first it was assumed that he was an unlucky victim of a nineteenth-century gold rush. However, there was a stone arrowhead stuck into his pelvis, which appeared to be Neolithic. Carbon-14 tests then gave him a date of around 7500 BC. This was far too early for any known gold rush, yet the physical type to which he belonged did not seem to resemble any branch of the Native Americans. He might have been related to the Polynesians, or one of the peoples of South Asia. Received wisdom has it that the Americas had been populated entirely by people of Mongoloid stock, who were the ancestors of all the peoples that Columbus and his successors had found there. Work on the bones was soon halted, however, when modern indigenous peoples in the neighbourhood lodged legal claims to the body, arguing that the bones could only be ancestral to them, or at any rate that more proof was needed. How could Kennewick Man be related to these peoples, if the scientists had identified his racial type correctly? The case became fraught and complex, because it raises big questions. To what extent do we own our ancestors? Are we sure we even know who these ancestors are? Nowadays, the number of Native Americans is small, and perhaps getting smaller. Does your need for knowledge outweigh my desire to maintain my identity, particularly if there are more of you than there are of me?

What do we really mean by the word 'ownership', at any rate in the case of inanimate objects or works of art? A man (they are nearly always men) may decide to pay millions of pounds in order to buy some flowers painted by Van Gogh, or a scribble by John Lennon, or one of Napoleon's teeth. He will then believe that he owns it, and in several ways he would be right. He will have pieces of paper to prove that he bought it from the auction house. He can choose which bathroom wall to hang it on, or which bank vault to let it languish in. He can prevent anyone he does not like from looking at it, or he can give it to his new girlfriend to win her favours. He can throw it on the bonfire on Fireworks Night to impress his children, although he may come to regret this when the tabloids get hold of the story, or the insurers find out how reckless he can be. But in practice this does not happen very often, and it is difficult not to sense that the so-called owner has merely parted with a huge amount of money in order to buy the right to look after the thing for a few years or, if he is lucky, a few decades. What he has really bought is temporary stewardship of the work of art, not the work of art itself.

In the case of a museum or art gallery, the stewardship normally turns out to be longer than this. The Rosetta Stone has already spent two centuries in the British Museum, which is getting on for a tenth of its lifespan. There are acts of Parliament which underwrite the museum's claim to own the stone, and there is no reason why these should not be respected. When a museum or art gallery takes refuge in the argument that something has been legitimately acquired by the standards of its day, and has been properly cared for ever since, this is not a trivial piece of special pleading; it is a valid appeal to our sense of fairness. This sort of claim can even be strengthened, when a museum returns other objects which have not been acquired lawfully. These may have been stolen in recent years, in which case they are regularly given back to the country which has illegally lost them, or they may have been looted in colonial times by way of reprisal or setting an overawing example to ungrateful natives. Concessions of this sort recognise that injustices can occur, and have done so on occasions. This can serve to underline legitimate claims rather than to undermine them. But even in undisputed cases, what we are really talking about is not out-and-out ownership, but a duty of care, since stewardship comes as the sister of responsibility. Is there a better way of looking at the problem than simply demanding our marbles back?

Even after three decades, I remember a conversation with an Egyptian colleague, an archaeologist who had become a respected journalist in Cairo. He said that, as far as he was concerned, Egyptian art belonged to the world, and for that reason he could not get worked up about the fact that there were Pharaonic sculptures in Canada or papyri in Copenhagen. It was the same with the many manuscripts and papers of British writers which are now housed in the United States. Rather than demanding their return, the British for the most part recognise that this is a tribute to the importance of English literature rather than an insult to their sense of self. It was time, my colleague said, to draw a line under things like that. Egypt was not in a financial position to look after all the treasures that were still in their mother country, so it was a matter of practical wisdom to put some of its heritage out to adoption. But it followed that, because Egyptian art belongs to the world, the world has a responsibility to look after that art, wherever it happens to be. Egypt is not a rich country, except in the sense that it is the heir to a rich legacy of art. Lands such as Britain and France, and others who have been entrusted by history with a share of that legacy, have a responsibility here, which is to help the Egyptians to preserve the part of that heritage which is still in the care of its original homeland. Cooperation is the price that comes with stewardship, and it is a price we should be prepared to pay, since it is also the way to deepen our knowledge.

Perhaps this is a thing the Rosetta Stone has been trying to tell us. In the hands of Champollion, this wisest of stones deciphered a chapter of our past. Today it may be helping us to decipher something about our responsibilities in the present, and our opportunities for the future. The schoolboy who first saw the Rosetta Stone in 1958 had the rare good fortune to be able to turn his hobby into his profession. Ten years later, as a student of Egyptology, I had the even greater fortune to see inscriptions coming out of the ground one morning, at a site in Egypt where we were excavating. They were covered with texts in a language I had never seen before. With me was the expedition's surveyor, a New Zealander who had the happy task of working in Egypt during the winter months and in Turkey during the summer. I asked him if he knew what the mysterious language was. 'That is Carian,' he replied, 'and nobody can read it.' The Carians came from the coast of what is now Turkey, opposite the island of Rhodes, and they settled in ancient Egypt as mercenary soldiers. Their language had defied attempts to read it ever since scholars rediscovered traces of them early in the nineteenth century. Here on the sand at our feet were some of their gravestones, which were written in their own strange language, and also in Egyptian hieroglyphs. The hieroglyphs we could read. The

25. 'The last farewell'. A Carian funerary monument from Memphis, now in the Fitzwilliam Museum, Cambridge.

texts were bilinguals, and these inscriptions which were lying in the sunlight that winter's morning turned out to be the Rosetta Stone of the Carian language. Trying to make sense of that language gave me a little of the challenge and excitement that Champollion must have known in his far greater decipherment of Egyptian, and it is one of the reasons which made me want to write this book.

Today the Rosetta Stone still stands in the Egyptian sculpture gallery of the British Museum. Its three registers were formerly highlighted in white to make the writing more distinct, but the chalk has been cleaned away, apart from one small area which has been left by the conservators. Millions of visitors view it, although many of them do so rather dutifully and briefly, before they turn to the labels on the wall nearby, which have the advantage of being in English. Some will know that a Frenchman used the stone to give rebirth to ancient Egypt, and a few may also spare a thought for Nelson and Napoleon, or perhaps Thomas Young. They may notice the extra inscriptions on the sides and wonder how George III came to be part of the story. Then they will probably turn away to view the more colourful and colossal pieces which ancient Egypt has given us, and of which we are all the temporary curators. They will buy their books and postcards on their way out. Some of them, like Champollion and his heirs, may be moved to visit the land from which it came, and which has given us so many of its treasures. If they do this they will, in a sense, be carrying the Rosetta Stone back with them, since it is the source which inspires all such visits and which acts as the interpreter to the civilisation which created it. The British Museum has given it a physical setting for the past 200 years, and it is a good home, but its true location is different and it is universal. That homeland is the wonder which is the beginning of knowledge, and which speaks to the mind.

THE TEXT OF THE STONE

This version is based on the middle register of the stone, the one which contains the demotic text. Some terms have been simplified or omitted, in particular the complicated list of magistrates which forms part of the initial dating formula, but otherwise the translation is complete. Some of the historical background to the text is given in Chapter 8. The translation is by the present writer.

Year 9, Xandikos, day 4, which corresponds to the Egyptian month Mekhir, day 18 [= 27 March 196 BC] in the reign of the youthful king who has arisen in the place of his father, the lord of the sacred uraeus-cobras whose power is great, who has secured Egypt and made it prosper, whose heart is pious towards the gods, the one who prevails over his enemy, who has enriched the lives of his people, lord of jubilees like Ptah-Tanen [the god of Memphis], king like Pre [the sun god], ruler of the upper and lower provinces, the son of the gods who love their father, whom Ptah chose and to whom the Sun gave victory, the living image of Amun, the son of the Sun, Ptolemy, who lives for ever, beloved of Ptah, the god manifest whose beneficence is perfect [Ptolemy V Epiphanes Eucharistos] …

On this day, a decree of the administering priests, the ritual priests, the priests who enter the sanctuaries to robe the gods, the scribes of the divine books and the scribes of the House of Life [the temple library and scriptorium], and the other priests who came from the temples of Egypt to Memphis for the anniversary of the accession of Pharaoh Ptolemy, who lives for ever, beloved of Ptah, the god manifest whose beneficence is perfect. These assembled in the temple at Memphis, and they said:

Inasmuch as King Ptolemy, living for ever, beloved of Ptah, the god manifest whose beneficence is perfect, son of King Ptolemy and Queen Arsinoe, the gods who love their father, is accustomed to perform many favours for the temples of Egypt and for all who are subject to his rule, since he is a god, the son of a god and a goddess, and he is like Horus, son of Isis and son of Osiris, who champions his father Osiris with a heart which is pious towards the gods, and since he has given great wealth and great supplies of grain and gone to such expenses to create peace in Egypt and to maintain the temples, and he has rewarded all the fighting forces which are subject to his rule. Of the taxes and dues which were in force in Egypt he has reduced some, and abolished others completely, in order to give prosperity to the army and the rest of the population during his reign. He renounced the arrears which were owed to the crown by the people of Egypt and all those who were subject to his rule, and which amounted to a generous sum. He released those who were in prison, and those who had been charged for long periods of time. He ordered that the endowments of the gods, the money and grain which are allotted to them each year, the shares which belong to the gods from their vineyards and orchards, and the rest of the property which had been theirs in the time of his father, should remain theirs. What is more, he ordered for the benefit of the priesthood that they need not pay their fees for becoming priests in excess of what they used to pay before the first year of his father's reign. He released those who hold temple office from the annual journey to Alexandria which they used to be required to make. He decreed that no sailor should be pressed into service, and he remitted the two-thirds share of fine linen which used to be produced by the temples for the royal treasury. He brought back to good order everything which had long lapsed from its proper state, and took care that everything which is done for the gods should be performed correctly. He also caused justice to be done for the people in the way that been established by Thoth the twice-great [the god of the moon and justice].

In addition, he ordered that those who had returned from the fighting, as well as those who had followed their own ways in the revolt which had occurred in Egypt, should be returned to their homes and their possessions restored to them. He took all steps to dispatch an army, cavalry, and ships against those who came to Egypt by sea and shore to attack it. He spent large amounts of money and grain to defeat these, in order to safeguard the temples, together with all who were in Egypt. He went to the stronghold of Lycopolis, which had been fortified by the rebels with every artifice, and with all types of weaponry and devices within it. He surrounded the fortress with a siege wall and moat, because of the rebels who were within, who had turned their backs on the orders of the king and the commandments of the gods. He cut off the canals which supplied water to the fortress, when previous kings could never have achieved the same. Much wealth was expended on this. He placed a consignment of infantry and cavalry at the mouths of the canals, to guard them and protect them, because the Nile flood was great in that Year 8, and these canals supplied great quantities of water to large areas of land, and were (correspondingly) deep. The Pharaoh took that stronghold in a short time, overcame the rebels inside, and slaughtered them in the way that the sun god and Horus, son of Osiris, did to those who had revolted against them in the same place at the beginning of time. As for the [other] rebels, who had gathered forces and led them to disrupt the provinces, doing damage to the temples and abandoning the way of the king and his father, the gods granted it to him to defeat them at Memphis during the anniversary of his accession. He impaled them on the stake.

He remitted arrears which were due from the temples to the crown up to Year 9, which amounted to a great quantity of money and grain. He likewise remitted the value of fine linen which was owed by the temples from that which is produced for the royal treasury, together with the audit fees [?] which had been charged up to that point. Moreover, he gave an order to renounce the artaba [bushel] of wheat per aroura of land [some two-thirds of an acre] which used to be collected from the fields of temple endowments, and similarly the wine per aroura of land from the vineyards of those endowments.

He performed many favours for the [sacred bulls] Apis and Mnevis, and the other animals which are revered in Egypt, more than anyone who had been before him had done for them, since he is devoted to their interests at all times, bestowing everything which is necessary for their burials, no matter how costly or splendid, and providing everything which is presented in their temples when the festivals are celebrated and burnt offerings made before them. All other things which it is appropriate to perform, the glories due to the temples and the other glories of Egypt, he established as they should rightly be, in accordance with customary law. He gave great quantities of gold, silver, grain and other riches for the shrine of Apis; he had it adorned anew, with work of the highest quality. He created temples, shrines and altars once more for the gods; he put other things in order, since he is at heart a god pious towards the gods. He sought after the glories of the temples, to make them new again in his time as Pharaoh, as is fitting. In exchange for this the gods have granted him might, victory and triumph, prosperity and health; and all other blessings for his reign as Pharaoh are secured for him, together with his children.

In good fortune! It has been deemed appropriate by the priests of all the temples of Egypt concerning the honours which are due to Pharaoh Ptolemy, who lives for ever, the god manifest whose beneficence is perfect, within the temples, and the honours which are due to the [preceding four Ptolemies and their queens]. A statue shall be set up to Pharaoh Ptolemy, who lives for ever, the god manifest whose beneficence is perfect, which is to be called 'Ptolemy who has guarded the Radiant Land', or in other words, 'Ptolemy who has saved Egypt', together with a statue of the local god presenting to him a sword of victory, in the temple, in each and every temple, and in the principal place within the temple. These are to be made in the Egyptian style, and the priests are to revere these statues three times a day, laying down sacred regalia before them, and performing all other things which it is customary to do, as is done for other gods at the time of the festivals, and the processions, and the prescribed days. There is similarly to be made an image of Pharaoh Ptolemy, the god manifest whose beneficence is perfect, the son of King Ptolemy and Queen Arsinoe, the gods who love their father, together with [its] shrine, in each temple, and this shall be installed in the sanctuary with the other shrines. When the great festivals occur, in which the gods are carried in procession, the shrine of the god manifest whose beneficence is perfect shall process with them. In order that this shrine should be distinguished, now and for all time to come, ten royal diadems of gold are to be added, there being a single uraeus on each as is normal for gold diadems, at the top of the shrine, instead of the uraei which are upon the rest of the shrines. The double crown shall be in the centre of these diadems, because this is the one with which the king was crowned in the temple of Memphis, when the rite of accession was carried out for him. On the upper side of the square which surrounds these diadems, and opposite the golden crown which has been mentioned, there is to be placed a sedge and a papyrus plant [emblems of Upper and Lower Egypt]. A uraeus is to be placed on a basket with a sedge beneath it on the right side of the top of the shrine, and a uraeus on a basket with a papyrus beneath it on the left side. All this is to signify 'the king who has illuminated Upper and Lower Egypt'.

The final day of Mesore, on which the birthday of the king is celebrated, has already been recognised as a procession day within the temples. The same will apply to the seventeenth of Mekhir, the anniversary of his accession. The origins of the blessings which have befallen all – the birth of the king, who lives for ever, and the inauguration of his reign – may these days, the seventeenth and the last, become festivals every month in all the temples of Egypt. There shall be performed burnt offerings, libations, and the rest of the things which are performed on other festivals, at both festivals in every month. What is offered as a sacrifice is to be distributed as a bonus to those who serve in the temple. A procession shall be held in the temples and throughout Egypt in honour of Pharaoh Ptolemy, who lives for ever, the god manifest whose beneficence is perfect, every year, from New Year's Day for five days, with garlands to be worn and burnt offerings and libations made, together with everything else which is appropriate. The priests in the temples of Egypt shall be called 'the priests of the god manifest whose beneficence is perfect', in addition to their other titles, and they are to write this on every document. They are to write 'the priesthood of the god manifest whose beneficence is perfect' on their finger-rings and engrave it on them. It is also permitted for lay persons, should they wish, to reproduce the likeness of the above-mentioned shrine of the god manifest whose beneficence is perfect, and keep it in their homes, to celebrate every year the festivals and processions which are described above. This way it shall be known that the people of Egypt pay reverence to the god manifest whose beneficence is perfect, as it is proper to be done.

This decree shall be inscribed on a stela of granite, in the writing of the divine words [hieroglyphic], the writing of documents [demotic] and the writing of the Ionians [Greek], and it shall be displayed in the temples of the first rank, the temples of the second rank, and the temples of the third rank, alongside the statue of the king who lives for ever.

FURTHER READING

INTRODUCTION

Most books on Egyptology mention the Rosetta Stone at some point, and the literature devoted to it is formidable. The short study by Wallis Budge which intrigued the schoolboy visitor was first published in 1913 and reprinted in 1922, the centenary of Champollion's decipherment. Its place has now been taken by a revised version by Carol Andrews, *The Rosetta Stone* (London, 1982). Those who feel the need to have the stone permanently before them can either buy a replica or consult Stephen Quirke and Carol Andrews, *The Rosetta Stone: Facsimile Drawing, with an Introduction and Translations* (London, 1988). The record-breaking postcard sales which the stone has notched over the years are the subject of an intriguing article, 'Souvenirs of Culture: Deciphering (in) the Museum', by Mary Beard in *Art History*, 15/4 (December 1992), pp. 505–32. An excellent short study, with good illustrations, is Richard Parkinson's *The Rosetta Stone* (London, 2005). The most detailed treatment of the stone and its part in the history of ideas is the same author's *Cracking Codes: The Rosetta Stone and Decipherment* (London and Berkeley, 1999). This is the catalogue for a full-scale exhibition held at the British Museum to celebrate the bicentenary of the stone's discovery. A vivid and well-balanced account of the work of Young and Champollion is contained in a work by two French scholars, Robert Solé and Dominique Valbelle, which appears in English as *The Rosetta Stone: The Story of the Decoding of Hieroglyphics* (translated by Steven Rendall, London, 2001).

CHAPTER I

The writer and traveller Lucy Duff Gordon is the subject of the biography by Katherine Frank, *Lucy Duff Gordon: A Passage to Egypt* (London, 1994). Her *Letters from Egypt* are edited by Gordon Waterfield (London, 1969). The idea that the flooding of the Nile was caused by a celestial teardrop survived into living memory, and a modern equivalent of the high Nile ceremony was described in Margaret Murray's *The Splendour That Was Egypt* (London, 1949), Appendix 4. The last hieroglyphic inscription from Philae can be found in Parkinson's *Cracking Codes* and *The Rosetta Stone*. The Coptic text in the tomb of Ramesses IV is published in H. E. Winlock and W. E. Crum, *The Monastery of Epiphanius at Thebes*, Vol. I (New York, 1926), p. 19; I was able to recopy it during a visit in the late 1980s. Okasha El Daly's *Egyptology: The Missing Millennium* (London, 2005) is an intriguing attempt to rehabilitate the writings of medieval Arabic scholars on ancient Egypt and its intellectual achievements. Other survivals of Pharaonic ideas and beliefs in modern Egypt are the theme of Anthony Sattin's highly readable *The Pharaoh's Shadow: Travels in Ancient and Modern Egypt* (London, 2000). The fullest introduction to what may be called the mystical approach to Egyptian is Erik Iversen's *The Myth of*

Egypt and Its Hieroglyphs in European Tradition (Copenhagen, 1961). Horapollo is best studied with the aid of G. Boas, *The Hieroglyphics of Horapollo* (Princeton, 1993). The polymath Jesuit is the subject of *Athanasius Kircher: A Renaissance Man and His Quest for Knowledge* by Joscelyn Godwin (London, 1979). The obelisk which he studied is described in Labib Habachi, *The Obelisks of Egypt: Skyscrapers of the Past* (London, 1978), Chapter 6. The attempt at translation which Kircher offered is quoted in Godwin, *Athanasius Kircher*, p. 62. Amusing accounts of Stillingfleete and Warburton, together with a perceptive analysis of Zoëga's contribution to Egyptology, can be found in Maurice Pope's *The Story of Decipherment: From Egyptian Hieroglyphs to Maya Script* (revised edn, London, 1999), Chapters 1 and 2; the satirical swipe at Egyptian learning given by Stillingfleete is quoted on p. 36. There is also very useful information in *The Legacy of Egypt* (second edn, edited by J. R. Harris, Oxford, 1971).

CHAPTER 2

The Battle of the Nile features in all biographies of Nelson, including *Horatio Nelson* by Tom Pocock (London, 1987) and *Nelson: The Immortal Memory* by David Howarth and Stephen Howarth (London, 1988). The most recent account is in Peter Knight, *The Pursuit of Victory: The Life and Achievement of Horatio Nelson* (London, 2005). The makings of modern Egypt are described in Gregory Blaxland's *Objective: Egypt* (London, 1966). A more heavyweight version can be found in P. J. Vatikiotis, *The History of Modern Egypt from Muhammad Ali to Mubarak* (fourth edn, London, 1991). A good treatment of Napoleon's Egyptian campaign is still J. Christopher

Herold's *Bonaparte in Egypt* (London, 1964), although there are many other accounts of the Corsican and his career. The man who brought the stone to England is less celebrated, but there is a memoir by Arthur F. Loveday, *Sir Hilgrove Turner: Soldier and Courtier under the Georges* (Kent, 1964). The colourful exchanges between the French savants and the British officers can be savoured in Solé and Valbelle, *The Rosetta Stone*, pp. 30–36, and in Parkinson, *Cracking Codes*, p. 21. The huge volumes of the *Description de l'Égypte* are best studied in the two-volume edition by Terence M. Russell, *The Napoleonic Survey of Egypt* (Aldershot, 2001). There is also a one-volume selection, with text by Gilles Néret, published by Benedikt Taschen Verlag (Cologne, 1994). Napoleon's Egyptian dinner service may be seen in the house familiarly known as 'Number 1, London', Apsley House on Hyde Park Corner.

CHAPTER 3

Thomas Young is not nearly as well known as he should be, even in his native country. This is no doubt because of the range of fields that he covered and the complexity of his thinking. The standard account of his life is the one by Alex Wood (completed by Frank Oldham), *Thomas Young, Natural Philosopher, 1773–1829* (Cambridge, 1954), but this is unlikely to be found outside specialist libraries. The same is even more true of Young's own *Rudiments of an Egyptian Dictionary in the Ancient Enchorial Character* (London, 1831). There is an account of Young's contribution to the understanding of the stone in Chapter 3 of Pope's *The Story of Decipherment*. Pope came to form a negative impression of Young, presumably as his admiration for Champollion increased. Exposure to some of Young's more jingoistic supporters will not have helped. This rather negative impression also colours the account in Lesley and Roy Adkins *The Keys of Egypt: The Race to Read the Hieroglyphs* (London, 2000). The version in Parkinson's *Cracking Codes* is more sympathetic, and corresponds with my own view. The extracts from Young's correspondence in this and the following chapter are all taken from Alex Wood's memoir, and some of them also appear in *Cracking Codes*. Young's letter to Bankes is reproduced in *Cracking Codes*, p. 32, fig. 12, and Parkinson, *The Rosetta Stone*, p. 37, fig. 15. The presidential address by the optician M. H. E. Tscherning is published in *Transactions of the Optical Society of America*, 23 (1921–2), p. 2.

Young has a walk-on part in the biography *Joseph Banks* by Patrick O'Brian (London, 1987), though here his importance may well be underestimated. An up-to-date biography of Young is badly needed, and this has now been provided by Andrew Robinson's *The Last Man Who Knew Everything* (New York, 2006).

William Bankes, the scandal-prone aesthete of Kingston Lacy, is the subject of *The Exiled Collector: William Bankes and the Making of an English Country House* by Anne Sebba (London, 2004). The Bankes obelisk features in Habachi, *The Obelisks of Egypt*, Chapter 5. Dava Sobel's *Longitude* was a best-seller when published in 1995. The same author has also published *The Planets* (London, 2005). Galileo's discovery, or non-discovery, of Neptune was announced by S. Drake and C. T. Kowal in *Scientific American*, 243/6 (1980), pp. 52–9, and followed up by E. M. Standish and A. M. Nobili, *Baltic Astronomy*, 6 (1997), p. 97. There are several websites devoted to the subject. Galileo was formally pardoned by the Pope in 1992.

CHAPTER 4

Champollion's life is justly celebrated, particularly in France, where he is a cultural treasure. The most detailed biography is by Hermine Hartleben, and was published in two volumes in German in 1906. This was translated into French, with additional notes, under the title *Jean-François Champollion: Sa vie et son oeuvre 1790–1832* (Paris, 1983). More recently there is Michel Dewachter's *Champollion: Un scribe pour l'Égypte* (Paris, 1990); this has particularly good illustrations. In English the most accessible work is Adkins, *The Keys of Egypt*. Pope's *The Story of Decipherment* gives a very clear and appreciative account of the man. Champollion's letters from Egypt are edited, with an introduction and afterword, by Peter Clayton, in *Egyptian Diaries: How One Man Solved the Mysteries of the Nile* (London, 2001). The account in Parkinson's *Cracking Codes* is also well worth reading. The Paris obelisk features in Habachi, *The Obelisks of Egypt*, Chapter 7. An illustrated edition of Champollion's *Grammaire égyptienne ou principes généraux de l'écriture sacrée égyptienne*, which was completed by his brother, Jacques-Joseph Champollion-Figeac, in 1836, was published in Paris and Arles (by Solin/Actes Sud) in 1997. A book by this brother is reprinted with illustrations under the title Jacques Champollion (*sic*), *The World of the Egyptians* (Geneva, 1989). Champollion's correspondence with Angelica Palli is edited by Edda Bresciani, *Lettres à Zelmire* (Paris, 1978, with a foreword by Jean Leclant). It would be good to see these letters translated, and the same may be true of other items in his literary output. Recently the decipherer has inspired popular literature of his own: for example, Christian Jacq's novel *Champollion the Egyptian* (translated by Geraldine Le Roy, London, 2003), which is based on the diaries of the Egyptian journey. The quotation from Champollion's letter which begins the chapter is the author's translation from Dewachter, *Champollion*, p. 117, and the extract from the *Précis du système* is a similar translation of the words quoted in Solé and Valbelle, *The Rosetta Stone*, p. 95. Many of the letters from Egypt are contained in Peter Clayton's edition of *Egyptian Diaries*.

The third edition of *Who Was Who in Egyptology*, edited by M. L. Bierbrier, was published by the Egypt Exploration Society in 1995. It contains entries on the two Champollion brothers, Young, Zoëga and many others, including the would-be decipherer Seyffarth. Letters and journals of several of Champollion's contemporaries feature in *Travellers in Egypt*, edited by Paul and Janet Starkey (London, 2001). The English consul in Egypt and his collections are the subject of *Henry Salt: Artist, Traveller, Diplomat, Egyptologist*, by Deborah Manley and Peta Rée (London, 2001). The diplomacy, or lack of it, involved in the early missions to Egypt can be seen in Ronald T. Riley, *Napoleon's Proconsul in Egypt: The Life and Times of Bernardino Drovetti* (London, 2003).

We know a large amount about Thomas Young and Jean-François Champollion, partly because theirs was an age of pen-and-ink correspondence which has been carefully preserved. Our century has progressed to emails and text messages, and we erase the signs of our previous thinking by exiting and saving the changes. How much of us will survive for later generations?

CHAPTER 5

The world's various scripts, including Chinese, are described in detail in *Writing Systems: A Linguistic Approach* by Henry Rogers (Oxford, 2004). The Egyptian writing system is the subject of Penelope Wilson's *Hieroglyphs: A Very Short Introduction* (Oxford, 2004; a reprint of the same author's *Sacred Signs*). The Near Eastern origins of our alphabet are traced in *The Early Alphabet* by John F. Healey (London, 1990). There is also much to be found in Pope's *The Story of Decipherment*, and Andrew Robinson's *The Story of Writing* (London, 1995). For the mysteries that remain there is Andrew Robinson's *Lost Languages: The Enigma of the World's Undeciphered Scripts* (New York, 2002). Lynne Truss's *Eats, Shoots & Leaves: The Zero Tolerance Guide to Punctuation* (London, 2003) contains information about pandas and writing. The quotation at the beginning of the chapter is the author's translation from text given in Dewachter, *Champollion*, p. 60.

CHAPTER 6

The story of Setne, the ghosts and the phantom woman can be read in Miriam Lichtheim's *Ancient Egyptian Literature: A Book of Readings*, Vol. III (Berkeley, 1980), pp. 125–38. The decipherments of Palmyrene and Sassanid Pahlevi, which are not well known in the English-speaking world, are described in Pope's *The Story of Decipherment*, pp. 94–9. The extract from Champollion's letter about chronology and the Church is translated from *Lettres à Zelmire*, pp. 44–5. Michael Ventris is the subject of Andrew Robinson, *The Man Who Deciphered Linear B* (London, 2002). The standard account of his work is still John Chadwick's *The Decipherment of Linear B* (second edn, Cambridge, 1967; revised 1992). Writing in the New World is the subject of Joyce Marcus, *Mesoamerican Writing Systems* (Princeton, 1992). The decipherment of Maya hieroglyphs is the theme of Michael D. Coe, *Breaking the Maya Code* (London, 1992; revised 1999), and is also described in Robinson, *The Story of Writing*. The revised edition of Pope's *The Story of Decipherment* devotes a postscript to it. The photograph of Knorosov with the magnificent cat is reproduced in Plate 24 of Michael Coe's book.

CHAPTER 7

The reconstruction of ancient Egypt's past in the nineteenth century is well told in Peter Clayton's *The Rediscovery of Ancient Egypt* (London, 1982) and Jean Vercoutter's *The Search for Ancient Egypt* (London, 1992). The latter is extremely well illustrated, as so often with this series. There are entries in *Who Was Who in Egyptology* on Brugsch, Lepsius, Erman, Sethe, Amelia Edwards, Labib Habachi and others. Fuller biographies of Griffith and Gardiner (the latter by his friend Jaroslav Černý) can be found in *A Century of British Orientalists 1902–2001* (edited by C. E. Bosworth, Oxford, 2001). Amelia Edwards's classic, *A Thousand Miles up the Nile*, was first published in 1877 and revised in 1891. Petrie is the subject of the detailed study by Margaret Drower, *Flinders Petrie: A Life in Archaeology* (London, 1985). Some of his correspondence is also published by Margaret Drower, under the title *Letters from the Desert: The Correspondence of Flinders and Hilda Petrie* (Oxford, 2004).

North American Egyptology is the theme of Nancy

Thomas et al., *The American Discovery of Ancient Egypt* (Los Angeles and New York, 1995). There is also an account of the growth of the Smithsonian collection by Ann C. Gunter, *A Collector's Journey: Charles Lang Freer and Egypt* (Washington, DC, 2002). A popular guide to the development of archaeology in Egypt is Nicholas Reeves, *Ancient Egypt: The Great Discoveries* (London, 2001). An excellent idea of the wealth of material from the workmen's village at Deir el Medineh can be gained from A. G. McDowell's *Village Life in Ancient Egypt: Laundry Lists and Love Songs* (Oxford, 1999).

A good impression of the range of Egyptian literature can be formed from Miriam Lichtheim, *Ancient Egyptian Literature* (three volumes, Berkeley, 1973, 1976 and 1980), as well as *Ancient Egyptian Literature: An Anthology* (translated by John L. Foster, Austin, TX, 2001). *In Praise of Learned Scribes* can be found in Lichtheim, Vol. II, pp. 176–8, under the title *The Immortality of Writers*. There are also two books by Richard Parkinson, *Voices from Ancient Egypt: An Anthology of Middle Kingdom Writings* (London, 1991), and *The Tale of Sinuhe and other Ancient Egyptian Poems 1940–1640 BC* (Oxford, 1997). The lament for the poor shepherd can be found in Adolf Erman, *The Literature of the Ancient Egyptians* (translated by A. M. Blackman, London, 1927), p. 131. For the historical side of things, a good up-to-date work is *The Oxford History of Ancient Egypt* (edited by Ian Shaw, Oxford, 2000). Also useful is Toby Wilkinson's *The Thames & Hudson Dictionary of Ancient Egypt* (London, 2005). There is much information to be had in John Baines and Jaromir Malek, *Cultural Atlas of Ancient Egypt* (revised edn, Oxford, 2000). The extracts from the letter of Sennufer and the epitaph of Kiya are published on the website *BBC On-line: Six Lives from Ancient*

Egypt (http://www.bbc.co.uk/history/ancient/egyptians/; translations and notes by the present writer). What is known of Princess Kiya can be found in Joyce Tyldesley's account of her rival, *Nefertiti: Egypt's Sun Queen* (New York, 1998), Chapter 5. An account of Tomb 55 and its many problems can be found in Nicholas Reeves and Richard Wilkinson, *The Complete Valley of the Kings* (London, 1997). Champollion's visit to the site of El Kab and the hieroglyphs of the song in the tomb of Paheri are recorded in Clayton, *Egyptian Diaries*, pp. 187–9.

CHAPTER 8

A translation of the demotic text of the stone, by R. S. Simpson, is included in the appendix to Parkinson's *Cracking Codes*, and is reproduced in the same author's *Rosetta Stone*. Another good version is given in Quirke and Andrews, *The Rosetta Stone*. This also contains a translation of the Greek and hieroglyphic versions of the text, and a transliteration of the two Egyptian registers. The text of the stone, slightly adapted from the various registers, can also be found on http://pwi. netcom.com/~qkstart/rosetta.html. Another translation is given on pp. 165–72 of the present book.

The best up-to-date account of Egypt under its Hellenistic rulers is Günther Hölbl, *A History of the Ptolemaic Empire* (London, 2001); the Great Revolt of the Thebaid, as it is often called, is the subject of Chapter 5, while Ptolemy V and the Rosetta Stone feature in Chapter 6. The Battle of Raphia is described in the fifth book of the historian Polybius. The wives of the Ptolemies, who were a feistier lot than their husbands, are the subject of Sally-Ann Ashton's *The Last*

Queens of Egypt (Harlow, 2003); Ptolemy V and his consort Cleopatra I can be found in Chapter 3 of that book. For light relief there is the fictionalised account by Duncan Sprott, published under the general title *The Ptolemies Quartet* (three volumes to date, London, 2004). A useful handbook of the better-known kings, together with their cartouches, is Stephen Quirke's *Who Were the Pharaohs?* (London, 1990).

CHAPTER 9

The question of Egypt's cultural heritage and what to do about it is explored in *Whose Pharaohs? Archaeology, Museums and Egyptian National Identity from Napoleon to World War I* by Donald Malcolm Reid (Berkeley and Los Angeles, 2002). There is also the provocatively titled *The Rape of Egypt: How the Europeans Stripped Egypt of Its Heritage* by Peter France (London, 1991). The influence of Egypt on twentieth-century art is explored in detail in *Egyptomania* by James Stevens Curl (Manchester, 1994). A convenient account of the Egyptian Supreme Council of Antiquities and some of the problems it faces can be found in Zahi Hawass, *Secrets from the Sand* (London, 2003). The extract from Frédéric Caillaud at the beginning of the chapter is quoted in France, *The Rape of Egypt*, p. 107.

The bronze horses of St Mark's are the subject of an extensive catalogue, *The Horses of San Marco Venice* (translated by John and Valerie Wilton-Ely, London and Milan, 1977 and 1979). The serpent column of Delphi and later Istanbul is described in *Pausanias: Guide to Greece* (edited with notes by Peter Levy, Harmondsworth, 1979), Vol. I, p. 441. The question of the Treasure of Priam and who should own it is the subject of the July/August 1999 issue of the journal *Archaeology Odyssey*. The complicated story of Heinrich Schliemann, Frank Calvert and the Treasure of Priam is told in Susan Heuck Allen's *Finding the Walls of Troy* (Berkeley and London, 1999). The Etruscan language, and the strange inscription from the island of Lemnos, is described in Robinson's *Lost Languages*, Chapter 5.

There is an authoritative website devoted to Kennewick Man at http://www.cr.ups.gov/archaeology/kennewick; this has links to many others. The issue of responsibility for cultural heritage is also the subject of much of Mary Beard's *The Parthenon* (London, 2002).

HIEROGLYPHS IN GENERAL

Hieroglyphs are a constant fascination and nowadays there are many introductions to the subject. One of the most user-friendly is Mark Collier and Bill Manley's *How to Read Egyptian Hieroglyphs* (London, 2005), and there is also Karl-Theodor Zauzich's *Discovering Egyptian Hieroglyphs* (translated by Ann Macy Roth, London, 1992). The elements can be found in *The British Museum Book of Egyptian Hieroglyphs* by Neal Spencer and Claire Thorne (London, 2003). More dedicated spirits can progress to James Allen, *A Middle Egyptian Grammar* (Cambridge, 2000), or even the third edition of Sir Alan Gardiner's formidable *Egyptian Grammar* (Oxford, 1957 and reprints). The next step is to buy a dictionary. The multi-volume Berlin *Wörterbuch* is unwieldy and expensive, but conveniently there is R. O. Faulkner's *A Concise Dictionary of Middle Egyptian* (second edn, Oxford, 1972 and reprints). Those of a more theoretical disposition will learn much from Antonio Loprieno's *Ancient Egyptian: A Linguistic Introduction* (Cambridge, 1995). There is a useful account of the writing system in general in W. V. Davies, *Reading the Past: Egyptian Hieroglyphs* (London, 2002). Penelope Wilson's *Sacred Signs: Hieroglyphs in Ancient Egypt* (Oxford, 2003) is one of the best and most original treatments of hieroglyphs and the thinking behind them. Orly Goldwasser's *From Icon to Metaphor: Studies in the Semiotics of the Hieroglyphs* (Göttingen, 1995) analyses the ways in which individual signs were arranged and interpreted by the Egyptians themselves. In a similar vein, there is the book by Barry Kemp, *100 Hieroglyphs: Think Like an Egyptian* (London, 2005), which explores the pictorial side of the writing system to describe the world as the Egyptians saw it. Learning demotic from scratch is not recommended (though Young and Champollion tried it), but students with some knowledge of Egyptian can refer to Janet H. Johnson's *Thus Wrote Onchsheshonqy: An Introductory Grammar of Demotic* (Chicago, 1986). Those with a penchant for Coptic can turn to Thomas O. Lambdin's *Introduction to Sahidic Coptic* (Macon, GA, 1983). There are many other grammars, but this one is up to date and well arranged. It is sobering to remember that Champollion and Young had no such aids.

The Egypt Exploration Society (3 Doughty Mews, London WC1N 2PG; website http://www.ees.ac.uk) sponsors research and excavation in Egypt and related areas, and has an excellent library. It publishes the annual *Journal of Egyptian Archaeology*, and also a quarterly illustrated bulletin, *Egyptian Archaeology*. It welcomes enquiries from potential members worldwide.

The Oriental Institute of the University of Chicago,

together with its outstanding museum, is situated at 1155 East 58th Street, Chicago, IL 60637. Its website can be found at http://www-oi.uchicago.edu. This URL has a link to the *Chicago Demotic Dictionary*, which is published on-line and regularly updated. The Oriental Institute publishes its own *Journal of Near Eastern Studies*, as well as a membership letter entitled *Notes and News*. It too welcomes new members.

LIST OF ILLUSTRATIONS

ACKNOWLEDGEMENTS

I am grateful to Andrew Franklin and Peter Carson of Profile Books for their patience, and to Peter Carson for his encouragement and kindly editorial advice. To Mary Beard, originator of the Wonders of the World series, I owe a wealth of additions and suggestions for improvement, all of them made when she was also chairing a sizeable university department and working on publications of her own. Michael Tilby helped me with enquiries about things French, and Annette Imhausen and Kate Spence with things Egyptian. Donald Welbourn and Stewart Cant, two Fellows in engineering, tried their best to explain Young's modulus to me: unsuccessfully, no doubt, but that was not their fault.

We would like to thank the Controller of BBC Online for permission to reproduce the quotations from the website *BBC Online: Six Lives from Ancient Egypt*, which appear in Chapter 7. Carol Andrews has kindly given permission to reproduce her photograph of the last hieroglyphic inscription which appears on p. 12.

The library of the Egypt Exploration Society in London has once again proved an excellent source of information as well as illustrations. The author is particularly grateful to its secretary-general, Patricia Spencer.

Sonia Falaschi-Ray came up with the translation of the words at the end of Chapter 4 that Champollion used to describe his daughter. She too had a go at the modulus. It was Sonia who made sure that I wrote this book, perhaps because she anticipated its dedication. During its writing she took on some of my quota of dog walks to spare my time. The dog appeared to be more sceptical about the project, and took to nudging my hand whenever I picked up a pen, but his decision not to chew up the typescript was taken as a gesture of support, and perhaps also of taste. He remains the Best of All Fellows.

INDEX

WONDERS OF THE WORLD

This is a small series of books, under the general
editorship of Mary Beard, that will focus on some
of the world's most famous sites or monuments.